THEotherAMERICA

Mothers on WELFARE

These and other titles are included in *The Other America* series:

Battered Women

The Elderly

Gangs

Gay and Lesbian Youth

The Homeless

Illegal Immigrants

Mothers on Welfare

People with AIDS

Teen Fathers

Teen Mothers

Teen Runaways

Teens and Depression

Teens in Prison

THEotherAMERICA

Mothers on WELFARE

by
Gail B. Stewart

Photographs by
Theodore E. Roseen

Lucent Books, P.O. Box 289011, San Diego, CA 92198-9011

Cover design: Carl Franzen

Library of Congress Cataloging-in-Publication Data

Stewart, Gail 1949–
  Mothers on welfare / by Gail B. Stewart; photographs by Theodore E. Roseen.
      p. cm. — (The other America)
  Includes bibliographical references and index.
  Summary: Uses first-person accounts of four women who are raising children on welfare to provide a look at the problems and concerns involved in this system.
  ISBN 1-56006-576-1
  1. Single mothers—United States—Social conditions—Juvenile litera-ture.   2. Single mothers—Government policy—United States—Juvenile literature.   3. Unmarried mothers—United States—Social conditions—Juvenile literature.   4. Unmarried mothers—Government policy—United States—Juvenile literature.   5. Maternal and infant welfare—United States—Juvenile literature.   6. Welfare recipients—United States—Juvenile literature.   7. Child welfare—United States—Juvenile literature.   [1. Pub-lic welfare.   2. Single mothers.]   I. Roseen, Theodore E., 1975-   ill.   II. Ti-tle.   III. Series: Stewart, Gail, 1949-   Other America
HQ759.915.S75   1998
362.83′92′973—dc21   97–43223
                                                                                                   CIP
                                                                                                    AC

Printed in the U.S.A.
Copyright © 1998 by Lucent Books, Inc.
P.O. Box 289011, San Diego, CA 92198-9011

Contents

Foreword

O, YES,
I SAY IT PLAIN,
AMERICA NEVER WAS AMERICA TO ME.
AND YET I SWEAR THIS OATH—
AMERICA WILL BE!
LANGSTON HUGHES

Perhaps more than any other nation in the world, the United States represents an ideal to many people. The ideal of equality—of opportunity, of legal rights, of protection against discrimination and oppression. To a certain extent, this image has proven accurate. But beneath this ideal lies a less idealistic fact—many segments of our society do not feel included in this vision of America.

They are the outsiders—the homeless, the elderly, people with AIDS, teenage mothers, gang members, prisoners, and countless others. When politicians and the media discuss society's ills, the members of these groups are defined as what's wrong with America; they are the people who need fixing, who need help, or increasingly, who need to take more responsibility. And as these people become society's fix-it problem, they lose all identity as individuals and become part of an anonymous group. In the media and in our minds these groups are identified by condition—a disease, crime, morality, poverty. Their condition becomes their identity, and once this occurs, in the eyes of society, they lose their humanity.

The Other America series reveals the members of these groups as individuals. Through in-depth interviews, each person tells his or her unique story. At times these stories are painful, revealing individuals who are struggling to maintain their integrity, their humanity, their lives, in the face of fear, loss, and economic and spiritual hardship. At other times, their tales are exasperating, demonstrating a litany of poor choices, shortsighted thinking, and self-gratification. Nevertheless, their identities remain distinct, their personalities diverse.

As we listen to the people of *The Other America* series describe their experiences, they cease to be stereotypically defined and become tangible, individual. In the process, we may begin to understand more profoundly and think more critically about society's problems. When politicians debate, for example, whether the homeless problem is due to a poor economy or lack of initiative, it will help to read the words of the homeless. Perhaps then we can see the issue more clearly. The family who finds itself temporarily homeless because it has always been one paycheck from poverty is not the same as the mother of six who has been chronically chemically dependent. These people's circumstances are not all of one kind, and perhaps we, after all, are not so very different from them. Before we can act to solve the problems of the Other America, we must be willing to look down their path, to see their faces. And perhaps in doing so, we may find a piece of ourselves as well.

Introduction

THE FACTS ABOUT MOTHERS ON WELFARE

The woman in the shelter did not want to be photographed, even if we promised that her identity could be shielded. "We can take your picture from the back, or in shadows," we suggested. But she was nervous, and afraid. What if someone recognized her, and they came for her children? Her words, she agreed, could be used, but not her pictures.

Connie (not her real name) is a twenty-seven-year-old woman living in public housing in the city. She has four children; their ages range from thirteen years to seven months. She was in eighth grade when she gave birth to her oldest daughter. Connie has been on welfare all her life; she cannot remember a time when she—or her mother before her—was not waiting impatiently for the familiar envelope with the AFDC (Aid to Families with Dependent Children) check to arrive. "I'm fourth-generation welfare, I think," she announces.

Connie's concerns are many. She is addicted to crack and knows her addiction is killing her family. She can go a day without the drug, but two days is inconceivable. The $1,102 each month she is allotted for food, rent, and bills goes quickly; she admits that much of it goes up in smoke—in her crack pipe.

"I'm praying I don't lose my kids," she says nervously. "I'm trying to get the courage to get into a [treatment] program, but I'm scared they'd take my baby away until I get straight. If I don't do good on the program and I lose my baby, I don't know what I'd do. But I gotta do something. The kids have been doing without for too long. I don't know where they're eating, I don't know who's watching them while I'm doing my thing with the pipe. I know they give me money to take care of them, and if I could get straight, we'd be okay."

"On the County"

Across town Lynn (not her real name) tells a very different story. She just turned twenty, and has year-old twin sons. Like Connie, Lynn refuses permission to use her real name or photographs, but not for the same reason.

"I'm from a very wealthy family," she says. "The whole notion of being 'on the dole,' as my dad would call it, is repugnant. Needing help buying groceries or paying my rent is a position in which I never envisioned myself. But at eighteen, when my friends were deciding which college they'd apply to, I was busy deciding not to abort my babies, and to live on my own.

"Now I'm trying to finish college, without help from my parents or the father of my children. The reality is, however, that even though I moved out of my parents' home to be 'on my own,' I can't do it alone; I receive AFDC and medical assistance. I get subsidized day care for my boys, too. A lot of the women I meet have known nothing other than welfare all their lives—they call it 'living on the county.' But I can't get rid of the feeling that I'm doing something really shameful."

A Hot-Button Issue

Both Connie and Lynn are "welfare mothers," women who are raising children alone with government assistance. Most women on welfare receive money to buy food and clothing for their children. They also receive medical assistance, which enables them to get free or inexpensive medical treatment. In addition, many welfare mothers are eligible to sign up for subsidized housing— apartments or houses that are rented on a sliding scale based on their income.

It sounds simple: Help those most in need until they can make it on their own without help. But as the case studies at the beginning of this introduction reveal, the reality of welfare is far from simple. In fact, there is a vast difference of opinion in the United States about the responsibility of government—federal, state, and county— to sponsor women, many of whom are mere children themselves, with benefits that allow them to continue being a burden.

"How much money should women with dependent children receive?" asks Tricia Clark, a Memphis social worker who assists single women on welfare. "Should we just keep handing over money, or should there be limits? If so, what should those limits be? Some people claim that by paying out more welfare for each out-of-wedlock child, we're encouraging these women to have more children. Others argue that if the government stops their payments, it is the children who will suffer the most, and we can't tolerate that. And of course, politicians get right in the middle of it, so it's become a real hot-button issue." Many point out that even with government support, children on welfare suffer from the lack of a two-parent, stable home and must cope with poverty, poor housing, and often drug and alcohol abuse.

THE ROOTS OF THE WELFARE SYSTEM

The idea of caring for mothers with children has not always been a function of government. In the United States public charity, or welfare, as it has become commonly known over the years, developed during the Great Depression, which began with the stock market crash of 1929. In the next decade 25 percent of working Americans were thrust into the ranks of the unemployed. Many who had enjoyed a comfortable living before the crash watched their children go hungry.

President Franklin D. Roosevelt instituted several programs, known collectively as the New Deal, to help create new jobs and aid the poor, sick, and elderly. Social Security and unemployment insurance, designed to provide workers with a "safety net" during retirement or in times of unemployment, served almost 3 million men in the depression. However, another group of citizens was also in need—and because they did not earn a wage, they could not benefit from Roosevelt's projects.

These were women who were raising young children alone. Most were widows; others had been deserted or divorced. During the '30s, middle-class white American women—unlike poor or black women—weren't expected to hold jobs outside the home while their children were young, in the belief that having a working mother adversely affected children. In fact, writes sociologist Jill Duerr Berrick, "keeping women out of the labor market was meant to protect children from the harsh realities of the outside world."

The government chose to give this group money rather than jobs, so that they could stay at home to rear their children. This program of providing a monthly check to women with children was called Aid to Dependent Children, or ADC, and was signed into law as part of the Social Security Act of 1935. The Food Stamp Program, which helped both feed the poor and decrease the huge surpluses of food stockpiled when depression-era farmers could not sell their crops, also provided help to poor women and children.

The number of ADC beneficiaries increased during the depression years, from 227,000 families receiving aid in 1935 to 527,000 in 1937. Even so, the ADC program was considered a fairly insignificant part of the Social Security Act, and attracted little notice as it continued to provide economic assistance to women and children during the 1940s and 1950s. (In 1950, the program was renamed Aid to Families with Dependent Children, or AFDC.)

However, the scope of the program changed dramatically by the 1960s. Surprisingly, although the nation was undergoing economic expansion and a decrease in total unemployment, the number of poor Americans was increasing. By 1969, in fact, 2 million families were receiving AFDC.

Eroding Public Sympathy

The civil rights movement of the 1960s and 1970s helped focus attention on the plight of a large segment of America's poor—American women and children who because they were black had often been excluded from welfare benefits. Before the civil rights movement of the 1960s, many states' regulations regarding AFDC called for ongoing surveillance of recipients to determine whether they were religious, morally fit, and possessed good housekeeping skills. Many states, especially those in the South, used the highly subjective examinations to deny payments to African American women. In the late 1960s and early 1970s many black women who were raising children alone pressed for benefits from various federal agencies.

The '60s and '70s was also a time when the composition of the American family changed dramatically. The typical ADC recipient in 1935—a widow or deserted mother raising young children— was gradually outnumbered. By 1971 only 4.3 percent of women receiving AFDC were widows; by 1991 widows numbered a mere 1.6 percent.

The "new" AFDC recipient was more often a woman who was divorced, separated, or never married. In 1950 these groups made up only 37 percent of AFDC recipients; by 1991 they accounted for more than 88 percent.

The changing profile of the welfare mother has resulted in a major shift in public opinion. Many see a vast difference between providing benefits for widows and deserted women to raise their children and providing benefits for mothers who have never been married. Because childbirth outside of marriage is often viewed with disapproval, if not moral outrage, the unmarried welfare mother on AFDC has become an object of criticism rather than sympathy.

"A lot of people are asking whether instead of helping mothers raise their children, the government isn't contributing to a breakdown in the family," says Lila Jeffries, a social service worker from Minneapolis. "So many single-parent families, so many babies being born out of wedlock. And it's the mothers who are blamed, I guess. The term 'welfare mother' has become a moral slur in our society."

Anna Lopez is herself a welfare mother, and she agrees that society's attitudes toward women in her position are more hostile than compassionate. "Nobody wants to admit they get help; people act like they're better than you. They call you 'welfare queen' or other names, and they say you have kids just to get more money. You know, a girl only gets about $70 more for each kid, and people think we do it for the extra money!"

The public's dissatisfaction with welfare is profound; in a recent *Time* magazine poll, 81 percent of people surveyed called for "fundamental reforms" in the system. Asked whether the current system encouraged poor people to work, 84 percent said no. President Bill Clinton made welfare reform a key issue in 1994 when he pledged to "end welfare as we know it."

CHANGES IN THE AIR

The welfare mothers of the late 1990s are single and young; teenage mothers form the hard core of the AFDC population, consuming $34 billion in benefits each year. Ironically, this is the segment of the population least likely to climb out of poverty. And it is that segment of the welfare population on which the system's critics are focusing their reforms.

The facts seem to bear out the dire predictions for these teens and their children. More than one-third of American babies each year are born out of wedlock, and those babies are seven times more likely to be poor than babies whose parents are married. Every day fourteen hundred teens become pregnant and decide to keep their child in the United States, over 66 percent of whom are unmarried. Of those young mothers, only 60 percent will ever receive their high school diploma. And without an education and the job skills that go with it, say experts, these mothers will be locked into the dependency of welfare.

However, the specifics of how to end that cycle of dependence are unclear. By 1997 new federal laws have limited the time that a woman may stay on welfare. Going beyond the new federal laws, many states have enacted their own limitations for welfare recipients, such as cutting off benefits for women who continue to have children while on welfare. Secretary of Health and Human Services Donna Shalala explains, "We're sending a clear message that we will pay for your first kid for a short time while you get ready for the workforce, but we will not pay for the second kid."

Clinton has his critics; some conservative politicians would rather end welfare to women and children completely, while many liberals feel that his plans are racist and classist. "If all welfare women were white, I don't think we'd be hearing too much about limiting the numbers of kids a woman can have," says one welfare advocate. "This sounds more like China than the United States."

PROTESTS FROM WITHIN

Interestingly, some of the welfare system's strongest critics are welfare mothers themselves. "It's a terrible system," says one woman:

> And people don't understand that we *want* to get off. I don't want to be on welfare, but I have no options. I didn't graduate from high school, so the jobs I can do won't even pay my rent, let alone shoes for the kids and all the grocery bills. But people act like they'd rather have me work and have less money. Without money for rent or other stuff, what would become of us then?

"I think lots of these conservative senators would be surprised to hear so many welfare mothers are as down on [the system] as they are," laughs another recipient. "But for different reasons. I'm all for limiting the time a family can collect welfare. But for God's sake, increase the payments so the family can get ahead! The payments are so small it's cheaper for me to stay at home than take classes, or even to get a job at McDonald's. I'd be in debt worse than I am now!"

13

And some recipients point to the indignity and humiliation they feel in asking for help. Jacqueline Pope, a professor of political science at Richard Stockton College, received welfare benefits after a divorce. She recalls her first days on welfare:

> I was very ashamed and also extremely angry with my husband for putting me in such a position that I had to ask for assistance. . . . [Going into the welfare office] was very difficult and the workers were so terrible to the people coming in. It was like they were literally opening their own pockets and taking out the money to give to you. And you felt so degraded by the whole process.

A Closer Look

The four women on welfare whose stories appear in this book are representative of the statistics. All became pregnant as teenagers. However, beyond that their stories are worlds apart.

Twyla is a thirty-five-year-old Native American mother of four. Like Erin, she first got into the welfare system when she became pregnant as a teenager. But though her oldest child is now nineteen, she does not see an end to her need for assistance anytime soon. While there have been times when she has worked to support her family, Twyla has not been able to stay off welfare. Her main complaint, she says, is that affordable housing is so difficult to get. "It seems like all they got available for you is these run-down places with bugs and rats, or heating or plumbing that doesn't work," she says. "And when you try to do the right thing and make the landlord fix what he promises he's going to fix, the place gets condemned or he throws you out for not paying your rent on time."

Erin became pregnant her senior year of high school. She comes from a middle-class family and says she knew nothing about welfare. She called "First Call for Help" in the phone directory, and was advised of the benefits available to her. Erin prides herself on having finished high school and held down a part-time job her entire pregnancy. Her son is now a toddler, and Erin is close to finishing her course work at a local community college, which she hopes will lead to a career as a police officer.

Jamie, a young mother of three, admits that she is probably trapped in welfare. "I read at a fifth-grade level," she says, shrugging. "Who's going to hire me?" She and her three sons live in a tiny cabin in a rural area; she is divorced from her husband, who was an alcoholic and drug abuser. Although she is not happy about her situation, Jamie feels that people should not be quick to judge her. "I've known some no-good welfare mothers, but I'm not one of them," she says. "Anyone who thinks my job being a mother isn't as important as my working in a factory or a store somewhere is crazy. This is just where I want to be."

Kathy is a thirty-four-year-old mother of four who has been on and off welfare since her sixteen-year-old was a baby. After years with an abusive husband, she is now single, and she feels she has been given a second chance. But although Kathy may be able to get herself off AFDC, her vision has become impaired to the extent that she will always receive another kind of assistance—disability.

Twyla

"ME AND THE KIDS ARE HAVING
A RUN OF BAD LUCK. . . . JUST
WHEN WE SIT DOWN AND THINK
WE'RE GETTING CLOSER TO
ACHIEVING WHAT WE WANT,
SOMETHING BAD HAPPENS."

Author's Note: I met Twyla and her children through a downtown shelter for homeless women. Although at first she might seem to fit the stereotype of a welfare mother—nonwhite, urban, jobless—she is surprisingly atypical. Although quiet and shy, she radiates a strong presence with her three youngest children, and when she talks about the importance of her family, the importance of the bond between herself and her children, I cannot help but be impressed. She has a good understanding of the curriculum offerings at various public schools around the city, and is very definite about which schools work and which don't. Twyla makes it very clear that she has no time for idle speculation about the future—her goals are day-to-day, and very well defined.

The neighborhood is busy on this early Saturday afternoon. Across the street from the park, several youths in baggy black shorts and cocked hats are hassling a man putting out garbage cans. He is shouting at them, and they are laughing and kicking at the cans he has carried from his garage. On the basketball court there is a noisy pickup game of two-on-two going on. Twyla and her three children are sitting at a weather-beaten picnic table, ignoring the noise of the game and the garbage can confrontation.

"Sometimes this is a peaceful place," she says. "I guess it's not today. I bring Freddie, my youngest son, here sometimes, since it's close to the shelter where we're staying. He likes to get out, run around. There isn't much space for that at the shelter."

Twyla gives the impression of physical strength, although she is a very small woman. Her black hair is cropped short, and she is dressed in blue jeans and a faded green sweatshirt. Her children sit wordlessly, as though they are used to waiting. The older boy slumps forward, his head cradled in his arms on the table. The girl looks at her mother, waiting for her to speak. Freddie, the youngest, leans tiredly against his mother, looking at me shyly.

"I've brought my three youngest kids—Rachel is twelve and Eddie here is fourteen," says Twyla. "This here is Freddie. My oldest is nineteen; she's got kids of her own. She doesn't live with me anymore, of course.

"We're on assistance, yeah. We get food stamps and AFDC. And medical assistance, we get that for when the kids get sick or have to get physicals for school or something like that. Also, the kids are requesting some Social Security from their dad. I don't know if that's going to happen or not.

"I've been on welfare a couple times, maybe three. On and off—I don't stay on it for long. Me and the kids are having a bad run of luck, here, though. It seems like just when we sit down and think we're getting closer to achieving what we want, something bad happens and pushes us down a hole."

"I'VE BEEN DEALING WITH THESE LANDLORDS"

Twyla coughs a deep, rumbling cough and continues.

"Our number-one goal right now is housing. I mean, we don't have much money, but we can't really do anything about that until we get a place to live. The last ten or eleven years I've been dealing with these landlords; it gets me discouraged. This is something a lot of people probably don't know, if you've never been in that position of being poor. It's nothing to be ashamed about, but it's a fact.

"See, if you don't have much money, and you can't afford a nice place, with rugs, and fancy furniture and things like that, you gotta look in the crummy parts of the city. The places to rent are cheaper there, because not many people want them. The plaster is broken, the windows don't shut right. The paint is peeling. And sometimes it's even worse—mice crawling around, cockroaches, bad plumbing or heating. So you talk to the landlord. You say, 'I don't want to rent this place, but I have to, because we need a place. But it's in bad shape. You gotta promise to fix it, though.' And the landlord promises to fix it, so you move in."

17

Eddie and Rachel, two of Twyla's children, sit patiently as their mother discusses the circumstances that forced her to go on welfare.

Twyla pauses, as though the silence gives emphasis to her words.

"But it doesn't work like that, not really. See, most of the time, the landlord doesn't have any intention of fixing whatever it is. Maybe he doesn't want to spend the money, maybe he's lazy. So the time goes by and you remind him, and then he isn't as nice as he seemed when you first moved in. And you are stuck, like me and my kids have been, plenty of times."

SETTLING FOR LESS

The problem, says Twyla, is that because she has always been so determined not to have her family land in a shelter, she has settled for poor housing.

"You move in, you need a place," she says. "You say to yourself, 'I don't want my kids living in a homeless shelter.' So you accept almost anything with a roof. But that's been bad for us, because we end up worse than before.

"You can withhold some of your rent, if the landlord hasn't done what he's promised. But then, he can file a U.D. against you—that stands for 'unlawful detainer'—which means you didn't pay your rent, so he intends to kick you out. That's happened to us. Lots of times the authorities believe the landlord, and you're out of luck. Sometimes it goes to court, and a couple of times I've won, meaning he doesn't get to kick me out.

"But I'll tell you," she says, picking at a thread on her sweatshirt, "that whole process takes so much time and energy, it ain't worth it. Even if they fix the place up, it's not much more than a dump, anyway."

NORTHERN ROOTS

Twyla glances at Freddie, who settles down, head resting in his arms, just like his brother. She nods in her children's direction.

"I don't want my kids to waste their whole childhood doing this," she says softly. "I had trouble myself when I was young, and it's a bad way to start out. I'm Native American as you can see—Ojibwe on my dad's side and my mom was from the Mohaves down in Arizona. We lived up north in Red Lake when I was young.

"When I was about four, my two little brothers died when our log cabin caught fire. One of the boys was eighteen months, the other only six months. It was a very sad time. I don't remember too much about it all. I remember my mom trying to run in to get them, but the smoke and the fire were too much, too hot for that. I remember the ceremony where we buried their clothes. There are these special plots up north, they've been for our family since the 1800s, I know. That's all I remember.

"But after that was such a sad time. We moved down to Arizona to my mother's people. But it was a different tribe, you know, different people. Different customs and ways of doing things. It was so uncomfortable that after a while our family moved back here, even though the memories were still raw."

ANGRY AND ASHAMED

Twyla says although it was something of a relief to get back to the familiarity of Red Lake, things were changing there for Indian people.

"It was getting really discriminatory toward Indian people," she says. "We moved into the town, not out in the country like before. But it was really different. Like if you went in a store or something, the salespeople would always be right behind you, seeing what

Twyla began receiving welfare when she became a single mother at age eighteen. Although she found a well-paying job, Twyla says she still needed some assistance from AFDC.

you were going to steal. That made me angry—angry and ashamed that I was someone people would suspect. And the police were bad, too. They would be pulling over Indians in their cars all the time. It was not for good reasons all the time, just because they expected they were doing something illegal. That stuff bothered me a lot."

It bothered her parents, too, says Twyla, especially her father, who was an influential man in the Indian community.

"He was real well known up north, really involved in a lot of political organizations to help Indian people," she explains. "In fact, he was one of the main founders of AIM—that's the American Indian Movement. You heard of that, right?

"He was so smart. People were always trying to get him to be a judge for the Indians, you know, because he was fair. See, back then when we kids were growing up, it was a hard time for Indian people, because there was a lot of anger about the fact we had so few rights. There was a lot of rioting on reservations, because people were mad at the way the government was treating Indians," she explains.

"I learned a lot from him," she says, thinking. "In the mornings he was an Ojibwe teacher at the high school, and in the afternoons he taught at the college. In fact, he used to get us excused for an hour each day from our school so we could come to the college to learn Ojibwe. He thought it was real important to be proud of your heritage, where you come from. That was more important than money, he said."

ON HER OWN

Twyla was just a teenager when she became pregnant with her oldest daughter. Although she had no relationship with the baby's father, by that time she was anxious to leave her parents' home and be on her own.

"I was eighteen," she says. "I didn't have such a good relationship with my mom—we fought all the time. My dad was sorry to see me leave, I know that. He was sick by then. He had bad kidneys and had to be on dialysis all the time. I think it was three times a week he had to go to the hospital for his treatments. My uncle even donated a kidney, but my dad's body rejected it.

"Anyway, it seemed right that I should be leaving. Most of my friends from school were leaving, too. Lots of them were getting married, having babies, moving to the city. That's what I did, too. I came to the city and stayed with my older sister; she already had an apartment here. I stayed with her about a week, then I found my own place. That was the first time I got on welfare, back then."

Twyla says that she signed up for medical assistance, which would take care of all medical bills for herself and her daughter. She also signed up for AFDC.

"The welfare for us worked like this," she says. "First I'd get a check in the mail at the beginning of each month. It was to help with food and clothes for the baby. I paid for the lights, heat, stuff like that. But I didn't want to stay on it that long."

A JOB, MORE CHILDREN

As soon as she could, Twyla applied for a job at a hotel downtown, only about twenty minutes from home.

"I was a housekeeper there," she explains. "You make beds, clean rooms, do vacuuming. I did a good job, though, and I could pay my bills and get off welfare. I worked myself up to supervisor, so the pay was really decent. Things were going pretty well for a while."

While her finances were in reasonable order, however, her personal life was becoming more complicated.

"I had a boyfriend all this time," she says. "It wasn't my oldest's father, no. I never had no other relationship with him after I got pregnant with her. But I met Edward because my older sister was married to his brother. We got along good, and we had kids—my three youngest are Edward's.

"I say that we got along good, but there were some problems. Now, of course, I look at things back thirteen years ago, and I'm disgusted with myself. I knew he did lots of drugs, but I figured things would change. You know how when you love someone, you figure that you'll be so good for that person that they will change anything bad about themselves? Well, that's what I thought. I thought me and Edward would be so good together that he'd stop drugs.

"But he didn't. And even after we had the kids later on, that didn't change him at all. He could be so good sometimes, but the drugs were bad, and I guess I was stupid to think things would change. They never did."

A DOCTOR'S DIAGNOSIS

Twyla says that she was still receiving some assistance for her children, but the amount was less than it was to begin with.

"I was making good money at my job, so we could live pretty good on what I made plus the assistance I was getting for my oldest, the AFDC. But then Edward started feeling bad, something was wrong with him. He was having seizures and everything; we didn't know what it was. I was thinking it had to do with the drugs he was doing.

"The doctors said different, though. They diagnosed it as epilepsy. That's a disease that affects your brain—that's why he'd been having seizures. You can't get a driver's license sometimes, because they never know when you're going to black out or something like that."

Stress seemed to make his condition worse, remembers Twyla, so she and Edward and her daughter moved back up north.

"The pace was slower up there, and we were around family," she says. "The city could be real stressful, with noise and crime and everything. As far as Eddie was concerned, we were better off, but I had to give up my job as a supervisor when we moved, and I felt real bad about that.

"After a while I got pregnant with Eddie—he's named after his father—and we moved back down to the city. I been here now ever since," she says. "The welfare money was more now, because Edward got disability. See, he couldn't work with his epilepsy, so the government gave him a Social Security check each month. That's called disability, what he was getting. That, plus what my daughter got on AFDC, and the medical assistance—we were in pretty good shape. I was hoping that when I landed a job, we could maybe start saving some money, even if it was just a little bit here and there."

HARD TIMES

Twyla was able to find a good job, one she truly enjoyed, and things worked out for a time, she says.

"I thought about looking for another housekeeping job, maybe working my way up to supervisor again," she explains, "but I

Twyla pauses for a pensive moment during her interview. Throughout her life, personal tragedies have interrupted her periods of self-sufficiency.

thought, that might take forever. So when this other job came along, I snatched it up. It was demolishing the inside of buildings. I did the demolishing; I was on the work crew. We'd take hammers and smash down the windows, rip up floors, smash the walls. I really, really enjoyed it—I wish I could find a job like that again. I was good at it, too, even though I'm built pretty small. In fact, I held onto that job for pretty near three years."

Twyla adjusts her position on the picnic table bench. She looks sad, as though these memories are painful.

"I would have made even more money, except I had to pay for a baby-sitter. Edward wasn't working, like I said, so he should have been able to watch the kids. But the drugs were getting so bad. He was never around. Sometimes he'd be there and he'd be so out of it, he couldn't even take care of himself, let alone the kids. And my job started at 8:50 in the morning, and I worked until 4:00 in the afternoon. It was hard on me, working so hard and coming home to Edward being like that. And I was resenting the expense of a baby-sitter—I mean, I had Edward just sitting around. I kept thinking, 'Why can't he help, at least with the kids?'"

The only thing good about that time, she says, was that she was off welfare.

"It gave me a lot of satisfaction," she admits. "For the first time in a while, I was paying for everything—rent, food, child care. It would have been nicer if me and Edward were getting along. But that's when I started thinking there was no hope for us at all. There was just too much bad stuff that he was doing."

A RELATIONSHIP DETERIORATES

Their relationship started unraveling as Edward's drug use and drug dealing increased.

"Things just kept deteriorating until they were so bad I couldn't stand it," she says. "He would be selling the drugs, doing them, it seemed like he was always taking off and going somewhere. We'd fight, and he'd get real violent. He would abuse the kids. I don't really think he even knew what he was doing. It was the drugs. That's no excuse, I know that. But when I talk about their father, I don't want them to think that he was intending to hurt them. He didn't.

"I ended up in therapy during that time," she admits. "I knew I had to break off the relationship. The therapy helped me figure things out. I mean, there were so many bad things then, and talking about them in therapy helped me to see how bad they really were. He'd go off to see his ex-wife, and each time she'd end up pregnant. He ended up having four kids with her.

"Another thing he did was steal our welfare checks, steal from his own kids. I was at work, and the AFDC checks would come in the mail, and he'd cash them all. That was the worst—taking money from his own kids, taking money that's supposed to be for their food and everything. Then off he'd go to get his drugs or whatever."

Twyla says that she and the children did not see much of Edward during the last few years they were together.

"He'd come around maybe two or three times a month is all," she says. "I was dealing with my anger at him, my worry about the kids and how they were handling it. And of course, I was busy working, trying to keep food on our table. We saw none of Edward's money. The money we had came from my job or welfare."

"IT'S HARD ON THE KIDS"

Twyla says that although she is furious with Edward for his actions, she has tried to keep most of her anger to herself.

"I don't want to spend a lot of time blaming," she explains, "because it doesn't help anything. I know it's hard on the kids to know that their dad was so bad. They don't like to think of him being that way. But they remember little bits and pieces, even though I pretty much keep to myself what I feel about him. Now Freddie, he was terrified of his dad, because he remembers his dad getting real mad, real crazy-acting, and shaking him up. It's still that way now, even though Freddie is ten. He still won't hug his dad; he doesn't want to touch him or even go near him.

"See, now Edward is really bad off. Me and the kids have spent the last three days over at the hospital, visiting him. Maybe for the last time, I don't know. He's getting worse all the time; he's getting some paralysis now, the doctors say. He came up with a medical emergency last week, and we've been over there a lot. He had a stroke, and two big seizures, one on top of the other. He's got pneumonia, too, so I don't think he'll last long.

"It's all hard on the kids, like I said. I don't get along with Edward, because there's too much bad history with us, but to the kids he's still their dad. I try to make sure they can spend as much time as they want over there with him. They like to do that."

LIFE WITHOUT A BATHROOM

Freddie, who had been dozing, stretches and gets up. He needs to use the bathroom, he tells his mother, so he walks over to the park building.

"Me and my kids, we had our share of hard times, more than our share. The last place we were at, it was pathetic. We needed a place, because the last landlord broke his promise about fixing up the walls to our apartment. So the city came in and condemned the property. In a way, I was glad, because the landlord shouldn't be able to make money off people with a place like that. But in another way, I was sad, because it meant we had less than thirty days to find a new place to live.

"So we came to this last apartment, and it was real bad. But we couldn't afford much, and we couldn't be living on the streets. So we said, sure, we'll take it, but you gotta fix the bathroom. The place didn't have a bathroom! He said he would—they always say that."

Twyla shakes her head, as though she cannot believe that they actually lived in a place without a bathroom.

Finding affordable, decent housing has been a major obstacle for Twyla. She and her children currently reside in a homeless shelter.

"We really did, we stayed there for a whole year," she says. "There was a big hole where you could actually see the next apartment. We had to go across the street all the time with pails to get water—I had a friend who lived in the handicapped building across the street. We used her shower, and then brought back pails of water to do dishes or have a bath, or whatever.

"Eddie helped; he was good about it. We lived like that, tried to tough it out, but it was too hard. We had bad mice problems, too, and cockroaches. It was disgusting—we'd try like everything to keep it nice, keep food picked up, but what can you do when mice are leaving their droppings everywhere, and the roaches are crawling in the drawers? It was that way when we moved in.

"It's maybe something other people with nice houses don't think about," she continues. "Or maybe they think that it's our fault, like poor people just *get* mice and cockroaches. They don't know that they are there in the place when we move in. And the landlords aren't on our side, not at all. They adjust the rent a few dollars, but that's it. That's something I bet lots of people don't think about."

"If You Don't Have a Home, You Don't Have Nothing"

Twyla says that she sometimes feels she is caught in a cycle that just keeps repeating itself: "Every time I've gotten a job, something happens to where I've got to leave it. If you don't have a home, you don't have nothing. It's like in Monopoly—you can't collect your $200 until you pass Go. That's how I feel. There are lots of things me and the kids need to do, but none of them can start until we live someplace, until we have real homes."

Why the plural "homes"? Does she envision them living in more than one place? Twyla nods.

"That's what we've planned. We've talked a lot, me and the kids. I'd be less worried about Eddie and Rachel if they'd go up north where their older sister Lisa lives, and stay there with her. I've talked about it with Lisa, and it seems like it would work.

"Lisa likes the kids, and they behave real well with her. She's just as tough on them as I'd be, and they know that. No fooling around, no hanging around with the wrong kids. No drinking, stuff like that. She'd crack the whip. And I wouldn't worry about them—here there's too much to think about with older kids.

27

Twyla plans to send Eddie and Rachel to live with their older sister, hoping they will have a better chance at success once they are out of the city.

"One of the things is their education. There's so many schools that aren't right, at least for my kids. Too easy, too few rules. I have had them in traditional Native schools, but I don't think they learn enough of what they need to survive today. In most of the public schools, they learn nothing of their heritage. Either way, they lose something, I think."

"I WANT THEM TO HAVE A CHANCE"

Twyla's own childhood up north has given her a good idea of what would be in store for Eddie and Rachel.

"They both like sports. Rachel is good at basketball, and so is Eddie. Maybe he'd be a good football player, too. I don't know, but I want them to have a chance. And here . . . I don't know. I don't want to sound like a racist, or one of those kind of people, because I don't think that I am. But here, it seems like it's all the black kids that take over the basketball courts. Around here, it's that way. They just chase off the Indian kids, or the others. It's not really fair. And I'm aware that life isn't always fair," she says, smiling rue-fully, "but with my kids I'd like to see the rules apply, you know?

"Anyway, up north, there's more Indian kids. There's more opportunities for them, and it's up to them to take advantage. I remember me and my family, we all did sports in high school. My brother Cornelius was in wrestling—I think he was in varsity for basketball from seventh grade on! That's good for kids, teaches them discipline and success. If they don't work hard with the opportunities they get up there, there's no one else to blame. So they can go to school, and have Indian teachers maybe. And play sports, and have a nice place to live with Lisa."

Wouldn't she get lonely without them? Twyla shakes her head, smiling.

"See, if I were sending them to live with some more distant relative, like a cousin or a great-aunt or someone, I'd be lonely," she explains. "But it's my own daughter. And so it's all family. Maybe they'll like it up there, maybe not. Maybe they'll come scooting back after a few weeks. But I think it's just what they need, and I'm going to let them go.

"Now Freddie, he's the one who is brokenhearted," she says, touching Freddie's head lightly as he sleeps. "He's crying already, because he knows it's coming. He loves these two, and they are real good with him. And no, I'd *never* let him go—he's my baby!" she protests, grinning.

"The other day, after we'd talked about it, Rachel and Eddie were outside doing an errand. Freddie comes home on the school bus—it drops him off right here at the shelter—and he thought they'd gone already. He was so worried they weren't here waiting for him at the corner. He said, 'Mom, do you think they miss me? Do you think they think about us up north?' And I told him, 'Ask them yourself at dinner, they're still here.' He was relieved! He doesn't want them to go until he can say good-bye."

A STRONGER FAMILY

Twyla has tried to pay attention to each detail of her children's move north. Lisa will be granted temporary custody of Rachel and Eddie, so that she will qualify for government financial aid in caring for them. But even with her preparations, Twyla says she is never sure what will happen.

"Every time the kids and I have a plan figured out, something comes along and interferes," she says. "Like I'm trying right now to get my identification papers. It's not a big deal. Just an ID, like everyone has. I had one, but it got stolen. So now what do I do? I go to the government center. I wait in lines, I fill out forms. But what do I put down for an address? My shelter? I can't do that. But if I need a job, I need to fill out papers, too. I have to show that I am who I say I am. But how do I do that without an identification paper? See how it goes in cycles? Plus you gotta pay money for this—I think it's up to $15 for the birth certificate now, and $12.50 for the state ID. That's a lot for me."

Twyla says that if nothing else good has come of her homeless situation, it has made her family stronger.

"The bonds between my kids and me are real strong now," she says. "I know that there's some damage there, with how their father treated them, and how he treated me. I know that you can't watch your mother get pushed around without having an effect on you. I know you can't get yelled at and screamed at and shaken by your father without having an effect on you.

"But the four of us talk a lot now. Rachel and Eddie know I'm not going to settle for a bad place anymore. Me and Freddie will get a place we can be proud of, and I can get us off welfare. That's what I want. And who knows, maybe Rachel and Eddie will come back and it will be the four of us again. Freddie and I can write them from a new house or apartment, and it will be a big surprise!"

"I Don't Like Welfare"

Twyla maintains that even though the assistance checks she has received through the years have helped, she doesn't like the idea of it.

"I don't like welfare," she says firmly. "Don't like it; ain't worth it for me. I know what people say—you get money, you don't have to do anything except sit around and cash the checks. But it makes us dependent on someone other than ourselves. That part is demeaning. I would never accept money on a regular basis from a friend, or from my relatives. I couldn't do that. I mean, if one of the kids was sick and I needed money for medicine, I'd ask. And my friends would help. But to ask, and then keep taking and taking—no!

"Then why should I feel any different about taking money from people I don't know? It's taxpayers, it's everybody. And if I think about that for a long time, I feel embarrassed. I should be looking after myself, after my own children."

Twyla says that she feels angry, too, that many people abuse the welfare system.

Twyla and her kids make their daily visit to the Department of Economic Assistance. Twyla derides welfare because it makes them dependent on the government. And, she maintains, "That part is demeaning."

"I see a lot of out-of-state people abusing the system," she says. "Sometimes they come up on the bus from Gary, Indiana. Or lots come from Chicago or Michigan. They get on welfare here, because our laws say you don't have to live here but a few weeks, I think, before you can collect. Well, some of those people are getting benefits that should be going to people who live here. That's what I think.

"And a lot of them aren't looking for a little money to tide them over. They're looking for a free ride. And so they get cheap housing, maybe rent it out to guys needing a place to deal drugs. That happens a lot. And in two or three months, there are a few more houses boarded up, crack houses closed down.

"We hate the welfare cheaters, too," she says adamantly. "They give low-income people, welfare people a bad name. It makes it hard for the rest of us when they cheat, or when they trash the houses. I've heard a lot of landlords say, 'Oh, I've had trouble with my previous tenants, so I don't do this or that,' or 'I have a policy against this or that.' It's all because of the cheaters. The system would work good if people just took what they needed and then stopped."

"ME AND THE KIDS JUST KIND OF SMILE AT EACH OTHER"

As for whether the new laws limiting welfare to certain people are effective, Twyla just shrugs.

"I haven't seen nothing different, and being in the shelter, you'd think we would," she says. "I see a lot of people coming in from other places, and lots of times they stop at our shelter first. Plus, you can't help but hear some of those ladies talking to each other when you're standing right next to them in lines, you know. They're talking about how nice it is here, how much they get, how happy they are to be here.

"I want to tell them thanks a lot for making it harder for me and my kids to find a place to live," she says, rolling her eyes. "They make me so mad. Plus, they all think this city is like heaven, they'll be getting a job, a nice apartment, whatever. I want to turn around

Filling out paperwork has become routine for Twyla, who spends most of her days trying to obtain housing, work, and identification.

and say to them, 'Lots of luck—you're living a dream.' Me and the kids just kind of smile at each other. We don't say nothing, though."

The prospects for a good place to live for Eddie and her are not good, according to Twyla. Anything that is in their price range (that is, what welfare pays for) is in a bad neighborhood.

"Lately, all we've seen for rent is a lot of crack houses or places right next door to crack houses," says Twyla. "I won't have that. You know that there would be lots of shooting, too. That's no way to live, especially for children.

"Not too long ago, before the apartment without a bathroom, we were living over near 28th and Bloomington. It's bad over there—prostitutes on the streets at all hours of the day, gangs everywhere. The day we were moving out of there, the police came by. There'd been a shooting, and they wanted to search our apartment building. I think they thought we might have had something to do with the shooting!

"That place was so bad, I wouldn't let my kids out during the day except to go to the school bus. People selling crack, people yelling and screaming at night, sirens. It was way too much excitement for me and my kids. It made all of us nervous."

THAT'S A DAY FOR US

Twyla says that one of the most incorrect assumptions about poor women, especially homeless women, on welfare is that they have nothing to do.

"That gets me mad in a way, but I kind of have to laugh," she says with a wry smile. "My days are busy, completely filled up. The bad thing is that the things I have to do are just stupid things, things that don't mean much in the scheme of things. Like, I'm not working, not going to school to learn something new. I'm not helping anyone else. I'm just doing the little jobs I gotta do to keep us in the shelter, trying to get my ID, stuff like that.

"But to say we don't have a schedule—man, if you could talk to my kids, you'd know we had a schedule! We get up early; usually that means 5:30, so we can get showers while there's still hot water. And we can do laundry without having to wait too much for machines. The kids help with that.

"We don't spend much time at all in the shelter, just mostly to eat and sleep. But we have breakfast, and we're out of there by 7:30 or 8:00. Freddie gets on the school bus, and for now, Rachel and

Twyla takes her children along when she goes to the government offices. "I figure it's good for them to see how much work it is being poor, being on welfare."

Eddie go with me; I got rounds to do, things that have to get done. For example, I gotta go over to the government plaza each day to get revouchered for the shelter. See, even though I'm allowed to be here for thirty days, I gotta get signed up each morning for that day. I put our name on the list so they know we didn't leave.

"After that I go to the housing office, see what's new there. We go and talk to my caseworker about whatever's going on—like maybe he hears about some new program or something me and the kids are eligible for. Something like that would be a reason to be hopeful, something to look forward to. But that wouldn't be all the time.

"I take my kids with me for all this. They hate it. They moan and groan," she says, smiling at Rachel, who rolls her eyes and nods emphatically. "They hate standing in lines the most. It's boring and it makes them tired. But I figure it's good for them to see how much work it is being poor, being on welfare. I don't want to do this anymore. I've never enjoyed it. And in a few days, they'll be heading up north to start school anyway, so it's not for too long.

"See, people take for granted a car, a house, an ID. But man, you don't have those things, and all of a sudden your day is real different. You're taking a number and standing in lines like me, standing around for them to call you. And yeah, it's boring. But that's life, at least for right now."

DAYS AND NIGHTS

There is one bright spot in their day, Twyla admits with a blush. She and the kids, no matter where they are and what they are doing at noon, try to get to a television.

"It sounds crazy," she giggles. "I watch *Days of Our Lives*. I never, never miss it, and neither did the kids during the summer. I don't even remember how we got hooked on it, but me and Rachel and Eddie, we're addicted. We have fun talking about the characters, wondering who will break up with who, and stuff like that. Anyway, we watch and we head back out, do more rounds.

"After that, I do some more errands, and then it's time for Freddie's bus. He has lots of homework—he's in fifth grade this year. Lots of math, I've noticed, and I've noticed it's a lot different from when I was in fifth-grade math! I have to work hard to help him, but he gets it done. He's a pretty smart kid, and he always tries his hardest. Once in a while, I have to get on him about his homework—he'll disappear away from the table, and he'll be playing with his cars in the corner or something. But mostly, he does good.

"We don't really have much going on once we eat dinner, except for homework. Really, we're all pretty tired once evening comes. In the shelter we have a little TV, just a small portable one that's ours. I have a big one, a 27-inch, but that's in storage until we have a place. I don't want to be lugging that thing around until we do.

"Anyway, we have a radio, too, and we listen to that. Mostly, me and Rachel read books, and Eddie and Freddie, they watch television or play Sega or something. Lately though, we just have been sitting around in the evening, talking. I like that a lot. We talk about plans, what we hope happens to us, how we'll feel when we're away. How we need to write letters and keep close. Sometimes we talk about things we did. I feel close to my kids when we do that; it's nice to have us there just talking quiet when it's dark. Sometimes they talk about their dad, whatever's on their mind. Sometimes I just feel real lucky when we're together like that."

Her kids feel a little lonesome for their friends, but she explains that that is one of the hardships of not having a real address or phone.

"When we lived in a real place, they did stuff after school with other kids," she says. "I think it's hard for them, being here. But Rachel and Eddie will make friends up north, and Freddie is more of a homebody. He likes being with adults, especially old people. He's got some friends he made all by himself—old people who really enjoy his company, and I think that's great.

"We go visit friends sometimes. I got voice mail at the shelter, and my friends can call. But there aren't too many kids around right now. But we have some friends that let us keep a few groceries around at their houses, so if we're out and about, we can make a sandwich and not have to go back to the shelter for lunch. The food is so terrible at the shelter, the kids consider a sandwich that I make a treat!"

"WE'RE SMART SHOPPERS"

Shopping is an occasional part of her day, and since her children seem to be growing a lot this summer, Twyla says that she has had to spend more than usual for clothes.

"Clothes is something I don't buy for myself much," she admits. "The kids don't want to dress in Goodwill stuff, and I don't blame them. I mean, there is no law that says that people on welfare have to look poor. We're smart shoppers. We watch the paper for sales, just keep our eyes open. Or my friends call me if they are at the mall and see shoes on sale or something they know we're needing. We help each other out that way. Who knows who's going to be high and dry next month—it's us now, but it could be them next, right? Anyway, I'm due to get my check Monday, so I'm going to buy a bunch of clothes and stuff for them to take up north when they go."

Twyla says that most of her welfare check has to be turned over to the shelter while they are living there, so she has less money than usual.

"It makes sense, I guess," she says. "We're eating our meals there, or at least most of them. And we're sleeping there. So there's no reason why the government needs to be giving us the money for those things.

"But what happens is that we are missing just the kind of 'everyday money' you just usually have. I need money for buses, to buy toothpaste and deodorant, shoelaces, lots of little things. So even though our 'basic needs' are being provided, there's a lot that isn't. I've borrowed a little from friends, but I don't want to get into a hole doing that too often."

"MAYBE SOON"

What about during normal times, when they are not in a shelter? Does she ever feel that she is getting ahead?

"Ahead?" she asks incredulously. "Not at all. If you mean, can I save any money, no. That's not possible unless I start telling the kids we aren't going to eat dinner from now on or something. If you mean, do I ever have any money left over at the end of the month, then yes, sometimes.

"Sometimes we have maybe $20 at the end, if we're real lucky. And yeah, sometimes we splurge a little—even though we have to cut corners pretty tight later—and eat out. We all have our favorite places, I guess. The older kids like gyros, those sandwiches with steak and onions. We went there sometimes in the summer. My littlest one loves Taco Bell, so I let him have that. Maybe once every six months we go to the movies, but that's too much money, really."

Living in a shelter has been difficult for Twyla's children, and she hopes they will be able to afford a home of their own soon.

Twyla insists that, when she is receiving assistance from the government, her attitude toward herself changes completely, and she hates it.

"There's just a nice feeling when you're not chained to welfare, when you're earning your own money, when you got a home," she says sadly. "You feel real good getting up each morning, because everything you do is for yourself and your family. You say, 'I'm going to clean that kitchen,' or 'I'm going to work,' or whatever it is. And you do it, and you're better off. But now, we're just doing little things to keep the cycle going, this stupid cycle we're on.

"I want to maybe take some classes, learn computers. I want a job where me and Freddie can go out to eat at a nice place once in a while, and I can buy some clothes that really fit me. Maybe that will all happen once we get a real home, with a real address. We'll get off this assistance and we'll be responsible to nobody but ourselves. Maybe soon."

"This is hard to say where you'll understand, maybe," she begins. "But mostly I miss a reason to get up in the morning."

Erin

"WELFARE IS SOMETHING I NEEDED TO KEEP GOING. . . . IT CUT MY SELF-ESTEEM A LITTLE—IT STILL DOES, TO TELL YOU THE TRUTH. NO ONE WANTS TO FEEL LIKE A LEECH."

Author's Note: Erin looks at herself as an atypical welfare mom; she admits she knows some who fit the negative stereotype many people have of single women who receive welfare while raising their children. She's the first in her family ever to apply for welfare, and if she has her way, she'll be done with it within another few months. She is grateful for the help it gave her while raising her son alone, but she sees it as a trap that could easily rob a woman of her freedom and self-esteem, and she wants no part of a life on welfare.

When the term "subsidized housing" is mentioned, the quiet, attractive suburban townhome in which Erin lives would not come to mind. Her two-bedroom home is set back from the road, surrounded by lush green grass and large maple and oak trees.

"There's a playground for the kids way over on the other side—but I'm glad I'm not living over there. Too noisy all the time," says Erin, a gregarious twenty-two-year-old with a ready smile. She and her young son, Cameron, live here, their rent, like many of their bills, paid for by welfare.

"NOW I'M ONE OF THOSE PEOPLE"

Inside the house is bright and clean, with a jumble of bright toddler toys stacked near the door. The youngster is asleep, she says, although she cannot vouch for how long the peace and quiet will last. Pictures of Cameron as a newborn, at six months, at a year, are framed and sit atop every flat surface.

"You ask me what I think when you say 'welfare mom'?" she asks. "Well, what I think of now isn't what I used to think of! I kind of look at myself. Before I started receiving assistance, I would look at welfare mothers as being this group of women who didn't do anything. They sat around eating, watching television, I guess, and having babies. That's the picture, the image that society has given us—me included.

"But now I'm one of those people," she goes on. "I can't think like that anymore, because it's personal all of a sudden. And so now I think of people who have a circumstance in their lives that makes things difficult right now. I'm a hard worker, and I think that the majority of women on welfare are like me. I mean, who in their right mind would want to be on welfare for her whole life? I can't even begin to imagine that!

"Some people might think it would be like being a kid for the rest of your life, that whatever you wanted, you could have, just like the government is this father or mother that hands out money. But of course, that's silly, because it doesn't work like that. It's not a deal where women are just hoping they can stay on welfare so they don't have to get a job or go to school or whatever. It's not like that at all."

CHECK TO CHECK

Erin insists that she views welfare as a necessary evil for her and Cameron right now.

"It's a bad thing to get used to," she says, carefully choosing her words. "I don't like it because it puts me in the position of living in a way I resent. I don't mean I'm not grateful to have it now, because of course I am. For me it's been a lifesaver. But I would never want to live like this for very long, being forced to live check to check.

"I know it's not just welfare mothers that live that way. Plenty of people who aren't on welfare have regular jobs but find it hard to get by and live check to check. But at one point in time, you just want to be able to catch up, you know? Most people I think have that freedom, and that's all I want. They want to say, 'Well, finally I don't owe any money,' or 'I'm done paying that off—that car or whatever.' Then they can save a little, or put some money away for

"I'm a hard worker," Erin says, "and I think that the majority of women on welfare are like me."

a rainy day. Maybe for a vacation, or for a house, or for their child's education. I don't think you ever really feel free until you can spend money the way you want. You know what I mean, right?"

SLIDING SCALE

Erin has not had that freedom for a long time, though she works long hours at a service station, where she is a manager.

"I'm trying as hard as I can," she says. "I work there three days a week while I'm going to school full-time this summer. But even if I have a month where I keep expenses down, or I earn more than usual, I pay for it. See, these townhomes are subsidized, which means the government helps pay the rent for them, so people like me, with real limited income, can afford to live here. The amount I pay is on a sliding scale, which means that what I pay is determined by how much money I'm making at the time.

"Now that works *for* you if you're having a real rough time, like maybe if your boss cut your hours, or you are between jobs for a little while. But it works *against* you if you have a good month or two. Then your rent goes up, and maybe you'll have less cash on hand. Rent will be more of a struggle to pay, and you'll have to pace yourself. That's happened to me—my rent goes up, but my income doesn't stay up. I guess you just have to learn not to get too happy when you have a good month, at least not while you're on welfare housing."

PREGNANT, AGAIN

Erin's experiences on welfare began when she was eighteen and found out she was pregnant.

"I knew there was no way I was going to be allowed to live at home with a baby," she says. "My mom had told me that before. You see, I'd been pregnant once before, at fourteen. That seems so young to me now! But it was a terrible mistake—the guy was eighteen. My mom and I talked about it a long time. She knew I had to get past it, that I had no business raising a child. I was still a baby myself. So I had an abortion.

"My mom and I got really close after that. I mean, she had always been the only parent for me and my brother. She and my dad had divorced when I was three; so she raised us by herself. She worked hard, and got some help from her family. She never used welfare. She might have been eligible, I don't know, but she didn't apply.

"Anyway, we got close. She became not only my mom but my best friend. We were really open with one another. I'd be there for her when she and my brother were fighting. See, he was always having trouble, drinking a lot, lying, stuff like that. He's okay now, but back then, he was a lot of trouble for her. That would draw me toward my mom, so I could be there for her. I wanted her to know that even though he was yelling at her, she didn't need to feel guilty or blame herself for his problems.

"We talked a lot about things, her and I. During high school, I'd had a couple of long-term boyfriends, and she'd tell me straight out, 'You be careful, now. You get pregnant again, and you'll have to raise your baby yourself—so you think before you do something you regret.' She told me that there was no room there for me and a baby."

"THE HEAT OF THE MOMENT"

Erin says that when she first told her mother about being pregnant, her mother was furious.

42

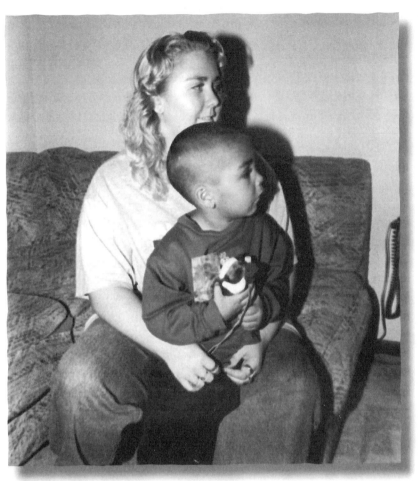

Cameron, Erin's young son, sits on his mother's lap. Erin first went on welfare after becoming pregnant with her son at age eighteen.

"She just exploded, and I ran downstairs," she remembers. "But it wasn't too long before she came down after me and talked. I know she was really upset. But she told me it would be okay, that things would work out. She told me not to cry, because crying isn't good for the baby.

"I didn't have as good luck with the father. His name is Ben. He and I didn't get along at all. We really never got along, now that I think of it. Deep down, I guess I always thought he'd try to pull something with me—that's just my intuition. He didn't seem real responsible, like he cared all that much about me. I mean, even after I was pregnant and was trying to figure out just where he fit into my life, he was so arrogant! He'd come over, leave some clothes—as though he was going to take his shower and this would be his little place to stay."

How did she ever let herself get pregnant by a young man she didn't like? Erin smiles ruefully.

"I *did* like him some of the time," she says. "It's just that he was kind of assumptive. It's hard to explain. It's just that I didn't like him as much as I wanted to. I think I got pregnant the way lots of girls do—not necessarily with a guy you love, just something that happens in the heat of the moment.

"Anyway, I was sort of back and forth, not really wanting to have a relationship with Ben, but at the same time I was wanting my life to work. See, every girl I know, they always say, I want to be married, have a good marriage, be with the baby's dad. That's how I wanted my future, too. I think at the time, I wanted it to happen, but I guess I knew that Ben and I really didn't have a future. But I needed support—I mean emotional support. I knew I'd have my mom and my friends. But it wasn't the same, you know?"

GETTING STARTED

So Erin concentrated on herself and her pregnancy, planning how she would live as a teenager on her own with a baby.

"I called First Call for Help, I think," she remembers. "I knew that I could get some assistance because I didn't have much income and because I had no one supporting me but myself. They told me about getting on some medical assistance right away, to take care of my doctor bills. And I needed some help with my food bill, but that was all. I would still work, so I'd be okay for a while.

"I was working at a pizza place when I got pregnant. That was a good job, but boy, by the time I was about four months along, the smell was really getting to me—it just made me sick, like certain smells do when you're pregnant. So I went over to the gas station, like four blocks away, and started working there.

"I didn't miss a day of work the whole time I was pregnant, you know," says Erin proudly, interrupting herself. "I didn't miss any school my senior year, either. I worked right up till the day I delivered Cameron.

"Anyway, when I went downtown to sign up for my assistance, the lady who was helping me put me into a couple of little classes—they teach you how to file for different bills, how to do everything the right way. They explain how the different parts of welfare can help you. And then after that, they gave me my medical assistance card, and I was all set.

"It's been really helpful," she says, nodding. "It paid for all the pregnancy and the birth. I got a big booklet, really thick, that told me which hospitals and doctors I could choose from, just like when you get insurance from a regular company. I was able to get a really good doctor and to choose a hospital near me, so it would be really convenient. To tell you the truth, I didn't really know how it would work out. For all I knew, they gave all the welfare people the hospitals and doctors nobody wanted. But that sure wasn't true!"

Erin also was enrolled in programs that supplemented her diet during pregnancy.

As a single mother, Erin is grateful for the welfare programs that allow her and Cameron to live comfortably.

"I got some money each month for my food, too," she says. "I have to tell you, it was kind of overwhelming at first, kind of confusing. Like, which program was this? What was I supposed to file? I got mixed up about it, but then I'd just call and there was always someone at the office that could answer my questions.

"I was put on WIC—that's Women, Infants, and Children. They paid for stuff that was really important to eat when I was pregnant—milk, cheese, eggs, that kind of thing. And when the baby was born, WIC pays for formula, milk, stuff like that."

"THAT'S REALLY A BIG DEAL TO ME"

Erin says that the most important part of the welfare setup is the caseworker assigned to each welfare recipient.

"She's the one you report to on a regular basis," Erin explains. "Like when the baby is born, you call her and she gets the ball rolling for the money for the baby, for all the new expenses. I can't tell you how important it's been for me to have a good relationship with my caseworker. That's really a big deal to me. She's the one that handles your personal case, who knows your situation. And if you have a good relationship with her, she's more willing to help you with anything, anything at all.

"See, there are a lot of people who complain about government caseworkers. They say how mean they are, or how crabby they act. I think that's because these caseworkers have to deal with so many people who try to get something for nothing, or who try to cheat the system. People act like they're entitled to stuff, just because they don't have much money. It's 'What can the county do for me now?' or 'How much can they raise my check?'

"And don't think people don't really cheat the system, because they do. I've known a couple of girls who cheat, and I don't even know that many people on welfare! They tell their caseworker they don't have a job, but they do. See, they just get jobs that aren't reported, just cash only, like day care or something. I know one girl who was working as a stripper in a bar. She was getting huge tips, too, so she was making a lot of unreported money.

"Anyway, I don't think I'd be pleasant most of the time either, if people were always acting that way toward me," Erin says. "I'd be anxious to help people who were really trying, who needed the help for a short time, who were trying to make a good life for their kids. So I try to have a good relationship with mine.

"Like, for example, I'm supposed to send in my pay stubs from my gas station checks each month. That's so they can check the amount I'm making and see how that measures up to my welfare payment. But if I lose one of my stubs, my worker will be less likely to make a big fuss and make me fill out a million forms to get duplicates and everything. She knows I'm honest, and she knows I have no interest in staying on welfare very long. She'll figure out a way around a problem, and give me a break."

ON HER OWN

Erin says that she and Ben didn't see each other much during her pregnancy, but that was all right with her.

"I did talk to him the day Cameron was born, before I went to work. He was in Las Vegas, and he called. I told him that in a week I was due to have a C-section. He told me he'd be back in time for that. I really don't know if he would have been or not, because we got in an argument on the phone," she remembers. "That was pretty typical for us. And as it turned out, I had the baby that very night.

"Ben wasn't there, of course. He came around a couple of times when Cameron was very little, but we really didn't get along that well. I wasn't looking for much with Ben, just a little support, a little interest in his own son. But one of the things that made me the maddest was that Ben acted like he didn't even believe that the baby was his. One minute he'd act proud that he had a son, and then the next minute I'd be hearing other people saying that Ben was running around telling people the baby wasn't his.

"I told him I wanted him to take a blood test to establish paternity, to prove it to him one way or the other. I had no doubt in the world, not one shred. Well, the test came back as I thought it would—it showed that there was a 99.9 percent chance that Cameron was his son. As conclusive as those tests go, yeah. That was important that the test was done, for any child support issues in court."

"I WAS JUST VERY NERVOUS"

Because she had no romantic interest in Ben, his lack of interest in her did not bother Erin. However, she still wanted him to have some sort of relationship with Cameron.

"I'm a firm believer that you don't have to be married to raise a kid," she says. "I think it's important to have a good relationship

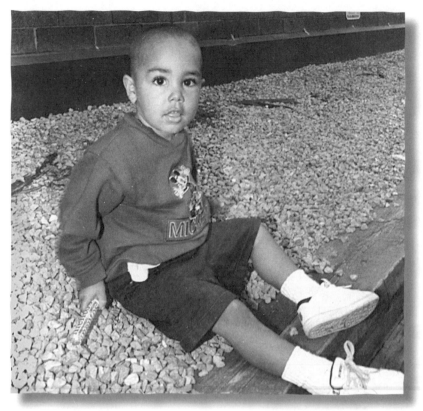

Although Erin is estranged from Cameron's father, she hopes her son will be able to develop a relationship with his dad.

with the father, but not necessarily be married. It's mostly important that Cameron knows that he's got a father and a mother, and both of us love him, that's all.

"So when Cameron was small, I guess I really was trying to make sure there was that bond between them, even though Ben was hot and cold about the whole thing. One time he had been over, and I had to go to work. I let him stay there to baby-sit; I thought it might be a good way for Ben to get closer to Cameron.

"Well, the whole thing backfired," she says. "My very closest friend—I think of her as a sister—called over there to my house to talk to me but talked to Ben instead. While they were talking, she could hear Cameron screaming and crying in the background. Cameron always had trouble with gas when he was tiny, and he'd get these major stomachaches. Anyway, with Cameron screaming like that, my friend felt like she should go over there, just to make sure he was okay.

"She called me, and I thought that was a good idea. It made me really nervous; I mean, Ben hadn't ever had to take care of Cameron alone, and with the baby so upset, I didn't know what would happen, you know? So she went over there, and she and Ben start arguing back and forth. Ben was mad because I'd let her go over there, like I didn't trust him. He called me at work—the whole thing was crazy—and I ended up coming home early. He was mad at me because he thought I had 'chosen' her over him.

"So after that, I didn't see him really at all. I heard he went back to Las Vegas for a time—I think he went back there to work as a dancer. I'm not sure, but that's what I think. When I did see him, he didn't really pay much attention to me."

A Bad Mistake

Although she was still working after Cameron was born, Erin says that she also wanted to continue her education. She enrolled in a nearby community college and began taking classes part-time. It was during her first year that she entered into a relationship with a man—a relationship that she says now was one of the biggest mistakes of her life.

"His name is Mike," she says. "He got so close to Cameron and me that Cameron started calling him Daddy. But this guy turned out to be very abusive, both emotionally and physically. And for a time, I was really trapped in that relationship, the way you hear many women become trapped. I'd get hit or punched, and I'd believe that it was all my fault."

It is not a subject Erin is comfortable discussing in detail, but she says that it was a horrible time for her.

"I thought he was going to be great. I allowed myself to dream that this guy was really right for us. But he wasn't. He beat me up once so badly that I was in the hospital—a minor concussion, bruises, minor injuries. He went to jail for that; as it turned out, it was his third offense. He'd done that twice before, beaten a woman up! So it was a felony, and as a result, he was in jail for three months."

A Good Ending

Erin says she never sees him now, and never wants to. After her ordeal, she was at a dance club with friends and saw Ben, however.

"He asked about Cameron, and I told him he was just fine. But then I said, 'No, he's not fine,' because Cameron was sad and

Cameron smiles after Erin gives him a push on the swing. Erin and her son are fortunate to live in subsidized housing where welfare pays the majority of their rent.

confused about Mike, too. So I told Ben I couldn't explain there at the club, because that wasn't the time or the place. He could tell something was really wrong, something bad had happened, so he called the next day.

"Well, we had a very good talk. I told him about how close Cameron had gotten to Mike and how stupid I felt about the whole thing. For a change, Ben and I didn't end up arguing. Our communication level was at a ten, instead of a zero. He said that he felt bad that he hadn't been there for me or for Cameron. He said none of this would have happened if he had been.

"Anyway, the really positive thing is that he's been a part of Cameron's life since then—in a big way. He's taken him on Fridays, taken him overnight. Cameron knows exactly who Ben is, that he is his father. Cameron was confused for a while, but he knows now. I still have no romantic interest in Ben, but that's okay. He's back in our lives as Cameron's dad, and that's the main thing.

"Another positive thing is that because of what I went through with Mike, I got involved with a battered women's shelter as an advocate. I put in forty hours of training to learn how to do it, so volunteering is what I do every Friday. It really makes me feel good to help other women get out of the same kind of relationship I was in."

FRUSTRATIONS IN FINDING HOUSING

What about the new welfare laws? Will reform affect her and Cameron?

"I don't think I'll have a problem," she says. "For one thing, I don't think I'm going to stay on welfare much longer. But I'm glad they're changing things, because I think people need to do more for themselves than they are doing now.

"One thing I hope gets changed is the length of time you have to wait to get into good housing. Like this place—we didn't start off here. I'm so glad we got in, but it wasn't easy, that's for sure. Cameron and I were living further away, in an apartment. It was lots noisier, not as close to shopping and my job.

"It's not that there aren't choices for subsidized housing—there are. If people think that all welfare mothers live in trailer parks or old, run-down places, it isn't true at all. Not always, anyway. I have a book from the housing authority that has addresses of places, and it's really amazing how many locations there are. It's frustrating, though, always going around filling out housing applications for these places, looking for an apartment that's in a good area, both for day care and for your job."

A LUCKY BREAK

The trick, says Erin, is finding a nice place, in the location you want, that doesn't have a huge waiting list.

"Places like this one are almost impossible," she admits. "I love this place. In fact, when I was in high school, some of my friends lived here, and I never knew there were units that were subsidized. See, not everyone here is on welfare or anything. Just some of the townhomes are, so people who want to live here put their names on a list, and the housing people call if there's an opening.

51

Erin studies for one of her classes. Because she does not want to remain on welfare, Erin has enrolled in college and hopes to forge a new career for herself.

"I had called about this one last year, but the lady in the office seemed really impatient. No openings, she told me, and the list was so long they weren't even taking any more names. But I got lucky, because my mom had a friend whose daughter was living here. I went with that woman, just went into the office, and she got the lady there to give me an application. The office lady didn't seem nearly as crabby as she had on the phone.

"Anyway, she told me that she'd squeeze my application in. The wait would be eighteen months to two years, though, so she told me not to get too excited. But I had a lucky break there, too, because I got a call in only eight months. We've never regretted moving here, not for a minute. In fact, when I'm off welfare, I'd like to stay here. This two-bedroom goes for $600 a month, I think. Right now, with my subsidy, I pay $155 a month. The lowest I've paid here, on the sliding scale, is $63; the most is $221. When I'm working again full-time, I'm hoping I'll be able to afford it; that's my plan, anyway."

"I'D HAVE A FEW IDEAS"

As for other changes in the welfare system, Erin says that from her personal experience she could make some suggestions.

"Yeah, I'd have a few ideas," she says. "I think the very hardest aspect of welfare for me has been trying to get day care for Cameron. I found out a week before my school started that I wasn't going to get help with my day care expenses. I just assumed that I would, since welfare paid for day care while I worked at the service station.

"But school, no. They told me that there was assistance only if I was working. It was terrible, and more so because of the stress of trying to find somewhere for Cameron with only a few days' notice. Luckily, at the last minute, I found a friend who said she'd be willing to watch him for $55 a week.

"But I really had it out with my caseworker. I mean, I knew it wasn't her fault, but I was so upset at how stupid the system was. If I had been on welfare for twenty-four months, then I would have been allowed money for day care when I went to school. It just amazed me! I was like, 'Okay, you people *say* you want us off welfare, but you only give us help for school day care if we've been on the system for two years. Why?' I told her that the point of going to school was to get a good career, so I'd never need welfare again.

"She understood," remembers Erin. "Eventually, toward the end of my first year on welfare, she looked at my record, and bent the rules a bit. She told me she was putting my name on the list early, because she knew I was doing my best and she wanted to help me out. So it worked out for me. I just think that should go without saying for every welfare mom—in the long run, it's the smartest thing the system could do, I think."

TRYING TO GET AHEAD

"Right now I don't get food stamps like some people do," she says. "I get one check, and that includes money for rent and food. But

Erin stands amidst the aisles of the Super America store in which she works.

it's itemized, so I know how much of that is designated for food, and I'm allowed an awful lot. It's just the two of us, and there's no way I can spend the money they give me on food.

"Now if this was food stamps, it would be going to waste, I guess. I think I'm budgeted for $220 each month for food for us. Maybe it's that I'm a bargain shopper, I don't know. But somehow, I just can't manage to use up that much money on food for us. So I'm glad I can apply whatever extra I have to other bills. So I'd suggest that maybe they should give more people the system they've given me—one check. Otherwise, there'd be food stamps going to waste."

She has plenty of other bills that she can use the money for, she says, shaking her head.

"My worst problem is cars," she moans. "I've got the worst luck in the world with cars. It seems like no matter how great the car was running when I bought it, it breaks down. And it's always something really expensive to fix, like a transmission or brakes or something. So, yeah, the money left over from my food budget usually goes to pay a mechanic.

"What I wish is that I could get ahead just a little bit. When Cameron was first born, I started a little savings account for him. I told myself—I *promised* myself—that I would only dip into it for real emergencies. But with the car and other things that have come up, I've got $23 in there now. I feel so bad about that. But it's just like I was saying before, about how it is living check to check. So I just have to think about the future, and promise myself that once I'm off welfare, Cameron *will* have a savings account, and things will be getting better."

"ALL I'VE EVER WANTED TO BE"

"I think a lot of people hold another stereotype about welfare mothers, now that I think about it," Erin says suddenly. "I think people assume that they've got no career choices, no real goals for themselves. I know that isn't true. I know other women like me who have big plans for themselves.

Car problems have plagued Erin, forcing her to spend her savings on necessary repairs. "What I wish," she says, "is that I could get ahead just a little bit."

Although getting pregnant while still a teen interfered with Erin's career plans, she is adamant that being a single mother will not "keep me from achieving what I want."

"I know I kind of got sidetracked when I got pregnant. But I never, never intended to just drift through my life after I started receiving welfare and after Cameron was born. In fact, I've had it all worked out since I was eight years old that I was going to be a police officer. My pregnancy has gotten in the way a little, but it's time to move forward now. It's certainly not going to keep me from achieving what I want."

Erin says that she comes by her interest in police matters honestly—her uncle and aunt, as well as her grandfather, are police officers.

"When I was eight, my uncle was working down at the county jail, and he took me through it and showed me everything," she says, smiling. "I just loved it—just everything about it. I liked the uniforms, the excitement, the way the police officers got along with one another.

"And then when I was fifteen, we had to do a sort of career report for school, and I got to do a police ride-along. Talk about exciting! It was just the best, and I'll never forget it. From that time on, a cop is all I've ever wanted to be, and I just know I'll never change my mind."

A Future on the Force?

Erin's hope is to be accepted into the criminal justice program this fall, after she finishes her work at the community college.

"I've been going to school, to college, almost two years now," she says. "I've actually got more classes completed than a lot of applicants do, so I'm hoping that will help my chances. Really, I plan to retake a couple of classes that I didn't get A's or B's in, so it looks better on my transcript.

"What appeals to me about being a cop is different from what I saw when I was eight, and what I saw later when I was fifteen," she admits. "I mean, it isn't just the uniform and the gun, and the excitement—although you've got to admit, the job wouldn't be boring. I think what appeals to me about being a cop is that the job is changing so much. Nowadays—around here, anyway—they're stressing the community aspect of it. It's not just arresting people, or chasing bad guys. It's walking through the neighborhoods, getting to know the people. Establishing a presence, so there is trust. I like that a lot.

"Everyone these days has such a bad outlook on police officers, at least that's how it seems. And I'm sure a lot of that is deserved. But I want to be one of the ones who shows people that being tough and mean is not what being a cop is all about."

What has been the reaction of her family and friends to her decision? Erin smiles.

"Well, I'm pretty sure my mom is fine with it. I think when I was young, she probably figured it was just a phase, and she didn't take me seriously. But now it's getting close to the time when I'll be actually entering the program (I hope!), and she's getting a little nervous. I can tell.

"My teachers have always thought it was cool, because it was so different from what other girls in my high school were thinking about. And my friends? When I got pregnant back in senior year,

I'm sure a lot of them were thinking, 'Oh well, there goes Erin's dream—she'll be a mom now and that's it.' But not me. I'd like to find them all now, and tell them!"

A FUTURE WITHOUT ASSISTANCE

Her need for government assistance won't end the moment she is accepted into the police training program, she says with regret.

"It's a school, basically," she says. "I mean, we learn procedure, shooting, all that stuff. We don't get paid as we learn, not like in some fields. But when training is over, and I get placed in a department, I'll be financially self-supporting, and that will be a happy day for me!

"I know people who say they feel sort of demeaned on welfare," she continues. "I know what they mean, because I've felt that way, too. You get treated differently by some people. Like when I went to the ear doctor, the nurse saw my medical card and I thought, 'Boy, I wonder what she's thinking?' It was just a little look, a little something about her expression.

"Or when I applied for financial aid at college. You do it by computer in this one room. This woman was going around helping people, answering questions. She looked over my shoulder when I was working at the computer, and she says, 'Are you on welfare?' Really loud—it was embarrassing. I just said, 'Yeah.' I know there was nothing to be ashamed of, but I felt bad. But then, I remember that people don't really know me, so they have no way to judge me. I have to keep that in mind.

"It's hard for anyone to accept that you can't do something by yourself. But welfare is something I needed to keep going, to get through a time that was hard for me. It cut my self-esteem a little—it still does, to tell you the truth. No one wants to feel like a leech, like you're having someone else pay for your food or your rent or whatever. But I'm working hard, and it's not going to be forever. And I'm not the only one, either. There are lots of other women out there, women with one or two kids, who are figuring out how to get on their own two feet. I say, good luck to them. And to me!"

Jamie

"I MYSELF AM DOING THE RIGHT
THING FOR MY KIDS. I'M A FULL-
TIME PARENT. . . . WHETHER I GET
ANOTHER JOB TO GO WITH THAT, I
GOT ONE JOB ALL THE TIME."

Author's Note: Of the four women interviewed for this book, twenty-five-year-old Jamie seems the least mature by far. With a very limited education—she says she reads only at the fifth-grade level—she seems to be in a cycle of welfare that has no indication of ending. She has three sons, ages nine, seven, and seven months, each with a different father, and is in the final stages of divorce from a man she says she likes but cannot live with. Because of her limited job skills (her best job, she says, was in a factory) she cannot envision a career for herself and is annoyed that anyone would hint that raising her sons is not a job.

The house is hard to spot at first, dwarfed by larger, newer homes on the lake. At first glance it appears to be an abandoned cabin, with little care bestowed on its yard. Packed dirt and a couple of concrete slabs take the place of a garden or lawn. But a second look shows that people are living here. A half-grown dog strains at a leash on the north side, a trio of kittens play just out of his reach. A red-and-silver bike lies on its side in the dirt.

There are television sounds coming from behind the tattered screen door. A towheaded boy holding a can of Coke is peering out, watching for visitors. As the car approaches, he waves shyly, then backs away from the door. A young, blondish woman in a "Miller Time" oversize T-shirt and blue sweatpants opens the door. "I'm Jamie—come on in," she says with a smile. "It's a dump, I know, but it's *my* dump, anyway!"

(From left to right) Dean, Dusty, and Richard—Jamie's three sons—provide ample distractions as their mother tries to concentrate on her interview.

"It Doesn't Seem Real Crowded Usually"

Inside, Jamie points to two young boys sitting on the sofa watching a big television screen.

"This is Dusty—he's the one that was standing by the door waiting for you," she explains. "And next to him is the oldest one, Dean." Both boys say hi but do not look in my direction. Their eyes are glued to a Boys 2 Men video.

The cabin seems even smaller inside. The main room, a combination kitchen–living room, is separated by curtains from two tiny rooms, one dominated by a crib with a mattress propped on its side against a wall. Jamie explains that she and baby Richard (now napping) share that room. The other room, containing Dean's and Dusty's beds, is a clutter of clothing, toys, and games.

"People who come in are always real surprised at how many people can live in here," Jamie says, pulling up a chair at the kitchen table. "It's nice for me and the boys—it doesn't seem real crowded usually. Today, with the rain, I guess it's going to get tight in here, because no one's going anywhere."

Dean walks over to her, brushing a handful of thick hair back from his eyes.

"Can I have a tuna sandwich?" he asks. "I'm real hungry."

"We can talk while I make lunch," Jamie says, pointing to a kitchen chair for her visitor, and taking two green-labeled cans of tuna down from the cupboard.

A History of Welfare

Jamie is on government assistance; she receives a monthly check of $950 to pay for her children's food, clothing, and assorted bills. Reliance on welfare is nothing new to her, she says, for her mother received assistance, too.

"My mom had me when she was only eighteen," she explains, "and my grandparents helped out a lot. And there were two older stepbrothers, my dad's kids from another marriage. But he wasn't around, so it was my mom and us three kids. We always had medical assistance and food stamps.

"My mom did the best she could. We stayed with my grandparents for a time when I was young, and they helped raise us. Things were hard for a single mom back then. I think it was from fourth grade on that we lived there with them. It was especially good having my grandpa, because he was really the only father I ever had. I never met my own father until after my grandpa died, in fact. But my grandparents were really involved. They'd go to the programs at school, the plays, the recitals, whatever. My mom did what she could, but my grandparents filled in all the gaps."

Jamie was fifteen when she first got pregnant; she admits that she started running with a new crowd at about that time.

"I can tell you why," she says, nibbling on a bit of the tuna. "My grandpa got real sick with cancer in 1986; he found out he had cancer. And I just fell apart. I started going around with different kids, going drinking, partying all the time. I was rebellious and angry; I don't remember exactly how I felt, but I wanted to get away from the house as much as I could."

"A New Kind of Bubblegum"

"It's funny, but my family didn't even notice the change. Maybe they were so busy with my grandfather. I'm not sure. A teacher at school suspected I was drinking, but when he mentioned it to my mom, she was in total denial. And I remember going to visit my grandpa in the hospital, and my grandma asks, 'What's that funny smell?' I'd been drinking just before I came in, and I know I smelled like booze. But I just told her, 'It's a new kind of bubble-gum,' and she bought it!

"See, I wasn't the type of person they would have suspected would get wild and drunk," she says. "No one thought I was that way. Even with the partying and stuff, I'd always be in by ten, my curfew. It was just what I did *until* curfew that was bad—even though they thought I was being good. But man, were they wrong! I was a fighter, too."

Jamie confides this last piece of information with obvious pride.

Following in her mother's footsteps, Jamie says she became pregnant with her first child while she was still a teen, thus beginning her reliance on welfare.

"I'd punch guys out if I didn't like what they said. I was a bully sometimes, I admit that. But I never hit a guy for no reason. I really punched out my boyfriend Gary at my grandpa's funeral—he had lit up a cigarette on the way to the grave. I belted him, and he felt it, too. I told him it was disrespectful to be smoking in a situation like that."

"THAT'S THE ONLY THING THAT SAVED MY BUTT"

Jamie knows exactly when she became pregnant, and feels very strongly that the hand of fate was somehow involved.

"I know how it sounds," she laughs. "But I was living so wild that I needed a wake-up call. If I hadn't gotten pregnant, I'm sure I would have drunk myself to death, or died somehow. But that's the only thing that saved my butt.

"I know I got pregnant the night my grandpa died. Gary and I were supposed to be out at this skating rink—that's what I told my family. But him and me, we took off to a nearby town to get some booze. On the way back to the roller rink, we had sex in the car. I told Gary I was pregnant, that I had just gotten pregnant. He told me, 'You're nuts—it's the booze talking. You can't know you're pregnant twenty minutes after you have sex.' But I told him no, I could just tell.

"Anyway, we got back to the roller rink, and the emergency call came for me, that my grandpa had just died. And that's how I remember the whole thing. Things kind of went downhill from there, though. Even though I knew I was pregnant, I waited until I had the pregnancy test to tell my family. My mom wasn't too shocked—I was surprised she didn't kill me.

"My stepbrothers, they took it hard. They were real protective of me, you know? Anyhow, we were standing out in the driveway one morning. My mom had this fancy new Bonneville parked right there. And I told my stepbrother Keith that we had to talk. He said, 'What's up?' And I told him, and he punched that Bonneville so hard, I thought his hand would go right through the metal! He was really mad, mostly at Gary."

OUT ON HER OWN

Jamie also told Gary, and his reaction was disappointing.

"He figured that was a good time to go into the navy," she says with a bitter laugh. "So I said, 'See ya.' I guess I didn't really care, except I hated that it all turned out just like my brothers predicted. They hated Gary, kept telling me he was never good enough for me, and then they turned out to be right.

"I stayed home until after Dean was born. I did write to Gary to tell him he had a son, but nothing came of that. Anyhow, I was really on my own with the baby, even at home. I had taken a lot of crap from my family before I had the baby. They'd say, 'Why are you going to keep the baby, Jamie? You know Mom will be the one to raise it. Why don't you put it up for adoption?' Stuff like that. But they were wrong; she never took care of him once, not when we were living there.

"I moved out when Dean was six months old. Mostly it was because my mom was really interfering, telling me what to do all the time. I couldn't take it. My aunt and uncle—they live in another town—they needed someone to baby-sit. I'd get room and board, so I thought why not? It seemed like a pretty good way to get off on our own, so we moved.

"Another reason it seemed like a good time to leave—I had been dating this guy Jerry while I was pregnant with Dean. He was divorced, had two kids from another relationship. I thought about being with him, but he seemed like he could never make up his mind whether he wanted his ex-wife or me. So rather than just stand around waiting for him to decide, I left."

SCOTTY, AND PREGNANT AGAIN

Jamie says that after she moved out of her house, she began seeing a boy named Scotty.

"We started out as friends; but there was some talk after a while of us getting married or living together. My aunt and uncle were supportive of him moving in. I was living at their house, but they were cool with the whole thing. I think they figured that they'd rather have me having sex in the house than somewhere else, some dirty motel or something.

"Anyhow, it wasn't too long after that that I ended up pregnant. And don't ask why I wasn't on birth control, either. Hey, I was on the pill back when I got pregnant with Dean, and I was on it when I got pregnant the second time. It's just the way things turned out, I guess.

"Scotty was actually happy about me being pregnant, at least at first. But after about six months, he'd start saying things like, 'Hey, I

Dean and Dusty put on their shoes and jackets so they can play outside. Jamie says that caring for her young sons is a full-time job, preventing her from working outside the home.

go to work every day; how do I know whose baby that really is?' That made me so mad! I just slammed my hand down on the table-top when he said that. And after that Scotty stopped coming around.

"When Dusty was born, I was convinced that I wouldn't be seeing Scotty ever again. In fact, I was already going out with another guy. But guess what? The night he was born, I get a call from one of his sisters. She says, 'Can we come over and see the baby?' I said yeah, fine. I didn't really know who 'we' was going to be. Well anyhow, a little bit later, in comes Scotty and his three sisters, wanting to see the baby.

"Scotty hadn't seen me in months. And he acted like he could care less. He asked me where Dean was, and I told him, 'Down the hall in the waiting room, watching television.' So he walks down there, buys Dean a pop, and that's that. A little later he comes strolling back to my room, tells his sisters it's time to go, and leaves. He never even looked at Dusty!"

NO SUPPORT FROM SCOTTY

"Over the years, I've called him and asked him if he'd like to come around and see the baby, but no. He never did. He always says, 'Sure,' but he never shows. Never an interest, I guess. But it was stressful for me, not having him around, because right after he was born, they found that Dusty had two little holes in his heart. Just the size of a dime.

"The doctors were hopeful that his heart would just grow together on its own as Dusty got older. But it was hard, thinking about that poor baby, and him having heart problems so early. It

Holding Richard, Jamie walks past Dusty, who is attempting to rig a fishing pole. Although Jamie says their small cabin is big enough for a family of four, she concedes that it can get cramped when the kids have to stay indoors all day.

would have been nice to have some support there, someone to talk to about it, you know?"

Dusty, hearing his own name, comes over to his mother's side. He is bored staying indoors, he says. Can't he just go out and fish or something? Jamie tells him no, and resumes her story. He leans against her, whining softly.

"Anyway, Dusty was on the heart monitor for a while, and Scotty was being a jerk. It seemed like everything was falling apart. I mean, I had welfare coming in for Dean and Dusty—financially things weren't too bad. But as far as *emotional* support, things were *real* bad."

Jamie recalls being very discouraged the day she and Dusty were released from the hospital. However, she says she had an unexpected visitor who showed up on her doorstep the same day.

"It was Jerry," she smiles, remembering. "He's the one with the ex-wife, remember? He was right there at my door, right after we came back. I was really worried, because Dusty had just got diagnosed. Anyhow, there was Jerry, telling me that he loved me and wanted to marry me!

"To make a long story short, we went and got married four days later," she says. "I mean, part of me was thinking, 'This can't be real; this isn't a smart idea.' See, he'd played this game with me, going back and forth between me and his ex before. So in a way, I didn't buy it. But deep down, I knew I loved him. I always had, but I figured he just couldn't get over his ex-wife, you know? I just thought, 'Well, you can't make someone love you back, right?'"

Marriage and More Welfare

Jamie's dependence on welfare did not end when she married Jerry. In fact, she says, they needed it more than ever, since Jerry rarely worked. What, then, did he do?

"What did Jerry do?" she repeats. "Well, he drank a lot, a huge amount of drinking. He did a lot of drugs. He could have been working steady, since he's a decent mechanic, but he just didn't have the self-control, you know? So he just kind of did nothing.

"I stayed on welfare with Jerry, at least most of the time. There were times when I'd get a job. I worked in a factory, I worked as a cashier at the grocery store, I did some housecleaning for a service. But really, it was mostly not working. I just couldn't get Jerry to get off his butt and work. So we got medical assistance, food stamps, cash to pay the bills. We moved into this place about six years ago. It used to be a cabin belonging to his parents. The rent was really cheap, so that was good.

"The thing with Jerry," she says, sounding a bit defensive, "is that it really didn't do any good for him to be working. See, he had those two kids from his ex-wife—actually it was three, since his daughter Heather was born just a few weeks after we were married—and he had to pay child support when he worked. And that was like $600 a month, maybe more. Even if he worked, it wouldn't be enough to keep us off welfare."

"YES AND NO"

Jamie admits that another important reason Jerry wasn't working for much of their married life is that he was in jail.

"For a bunch of different reasons," she says. "Driving after his license was revoked, stealing snowmobiles, stuff like that. He had no judgment, I think that was his main problem."

Did she ever stop to figure out why she was involved with so many young men who were, for all intents and purposes, losers? Does she see a pattern in her life of settling for relationships with men who had serious problems?

"Yes and no," she says, shaking her hair back from her face. "I know to someone else, it sounds like these guys were just bad news, but that's not completely the case. I mean, with Gary, the whole thing is just that we were very young. But in a way, that was a good thing, because like I said, if I hadn't have gotten pregnant with Dean, I'd have been dead, right? So that's Gary. And with Scotty—I'm not really sure about him. I think we could have stayed friends, but he didn't have it in him to be committed. I think he was just used to getting what he wanted—he was the baby of his family. And Jerry? Just back and forth with the ex, I guess. He buckled under from the pressure, maybe.

"I know I got angry with him. I just didn't take it without giving a little back. I mean, one day I'd come home early from the factory—they let us out early on Fridays. And my friend stopped by to see me, and she says, 'Jamie, you know, they're all doing crank down in your basement.' I say, 'Crank? Like the drug crank?' And she says yeah, a bunch of them are down in the basement doing it. So I looked right at her, and I said, 'I'll be right back.'

"I walked outside and I just went nuts. I yelled. Everyone who knows me knows that when I'm mad I holler. I stormed out to the basement door (our basement has an outside entrance) and I just screamed, 'Will everybody please get out of here except Jerry.' So they all scattered; they were scared to death of me. Then Jerry asks me, 'What'd I do?' I asked him in a pretty calm voice what he was doing down there, and he told me nothing.

"Well, I got sick of that back and forth stuff, and I said, 'I'm giving you three seconds and then I'm bouncing your head off the wall.' He says, 'Oh, Jamie, we've just been cranking a little bit, no big deal.' So I told him no way, that it was illegal, it was bad. And I went outside and I said, 'Okay, all you druggies, get out of my house, get away from my property!' And that was that, I guess."

In Jail

Jamie says that one of the reasons she was so angry was that they'd been married for four years, and she had no idea that he was using such strong drugs.

Jamie says that the men in her life did nothing to help her get off welfare. Even when she was working, she could not make enough money to support her family without the help of welfare.

69

"I knew he drank," she says. "And I knew he smoked a lot of weed, but I didn't think he was into anything as heavy as crank. I mean, if the cops had come, we could have lost our house, the kids, who knows? He had no business putting what we had in that kind of jeopardy.

"Anyhow, the next weekend, Jerry goes up north with some of his friends. They liked snowmobiling, stuff like that. And I got a call from him, from jail. He told me that they'd arrested him for stealing some guy's snowmobile. I told him not to bother coming home if he ever got out of jail.

"I got me a baby-sitter to watch the two boys," she remembers. "And I went up north, to find out what was going on. I stayed with my mom—she lives like half an hour from the town where he was in jail. It was really embarrassing, too, because the story was in the paper up there. Everyone knew what a dumb thing he'd done."

Jamie says that after Jerry was released from jail, she took her two boys and moved up north.

"I really didn't want anything to do with him after that," she says. "I had a place to live near my mom's house, and that was fine. I even started going out with a guy up there—I figured I was sort of unattached, and it wasn't serious, anyway.

"This guy's name was David; he was a friend of my brother's. I laughed when he asked me to dinner; I thought, what kind of a guy would want to go out with someone with two kids? But we went out, and I sort of liked him. I had heard from Jerry that he was filing for divorce. He said he wanted the house. It didn't really bother me that he did that, as long as I had my boys.

"But then something came up—I became pregnant," she laughs. "It was David's baby, yeah. And I found out something interesting. David was like the others. He just took off and split. He didn't want nothing to do with me being pregnant, I guess."

ANOTHER CHANCE

Being on her own with two small children and a baby on the way put Jamie in a difficult position. Although she had said she didn't want to have anything more to do with Jerry, they met and talked.

"He said he loved me," she says. "He was upset with me for abandoning him when he was in jail, just taking off. But he said he loved me. He had stopped drinking and using, and he thought

70

maybe we should give our marriage one more try. I thought about it, and I agreed.

"He did a good job, too. He coached me through labor and delivery of the baby—Richard. He put his name on Richard's birth certificate as the father. He was good with the other boys, acted just like a father, especially now that he wasn't drinking or using drugs."

However, in a few months Jamie and Jerry started running into trouble. Although he had not begun drinking again, Jerry had entered a "dry drunk" stage, says Jamie.

"Dry drunk is like even though you aren't drinking, you act drunk," she explains. "And I didn't see it ending anytime soon. He was verbally abusive to me. Never the kids, I'll give him that. But he'd say things to me like how fat I was, or how wide my ass was getting. I wanted to rip his head off, if you know the truth. I'd tell him, 'Hey, you can't love me fat, you can't love me skinny, either.' Anyway, it was one thing after another, one fight right on top of another one.

"So we sat down and decided that it was over between us. We care about each other, but we can't be together. It doesn't work. We had discussions about who would get the house, who would have to move out. The boys were sad, because Jerry's the only father they've ever known, but we both agreed that that would continue. You can't deprive kids of their father. So me and Jerry got divorced—we're just in the final stages now."

THE TROUBLE WITH THE SYSTEM

Jamie says that she has real financial worries now that she is on her own with three small children.

"I'm not getting anything from Jerry," she says. "He's still not working, or if he is, it's not much. He tries to help me by watching the kids sometimes, but he has his own life, too. He goes to AA [Alcoholics Anonymous] meetings pretty near every day. He's got stuff to do. And like I said before, the minute he works, he's got child support from his ex to pay. So there's not much help coming from him, at least not in the form of money or anything like that.

"See, I talked to Jerry just a little bit ago about my working this summer. I wanted to get a job, maybe go back to the factory. He lives just a few miles away, so I was hoping he'd watch the boys. Anyway, I told him about the idea of working, and he says,

Jamie maintains that part of the reason she does not go back to work is because she is particular about who she will let watch her sons. "I don't feel like I should have to go to work if I don't feel comfortable about who is watching them," she asserts.

'Working? Are you sure you can afford to do that? I can help out a little bit, but don't count on me all the time.' So, since he couldn't help out all the time, I sure can't afford it."

But doesn't welfare pay for her child care when she works? Jamie shrugs.

"Yes and no," she says. "I don't want my kids watched by just anybody. And they have a rule at the welfare office that unless you get someone to do day care that's in their books, that's certified with them, they won't pay a nickel. And that's not easy, I'm telling you.

"When Dean and Dusty were little, I tried to go back to work every now and again, and I always tried to have someone watch them that I trusted. You don't know who's going to be decent to them. I don't feel like I should have to go to work if I don't feel comfortable about who is watching them, right?

"Like when fall starts, I'm going job hunting. Before school starts, I can't really make enough, not with all three of them being watched. Dean and Dusty will be in school, so it will just be

Richard that needs the care. The county would pay, and that's a great theory, but who have they got for accredited child care?

"There's a lady across the lake; she's got six kids of her own. She's had Dean over there, playing with her son after school. When I came to pick him up, he didn't want to come home! They've turned their whole basement into a roller rink, and the kids are downstairs just having a ball. I mean, who wouldn't like to be there? There's wall-to-wall kids, and stuff to do. She'll do day care—I asked her about it. But the county won't pay for it, because she's not accredited. That's the system; it's not set up right."

WHY SHOULD TAXPAYERS PAY FOR HER WELFARE?

But why should the system pay for her and for Jerry to not work? Why should it be easy to have children but to have no way to support them? Jamie's smile fades a bit.

"I'm not the problem, though," she says defensively. "It's these women who keep having babies just to get the money. I know there are a lot of women like that. These young moms think, 'I'll just have another kid and we'll get some money.' Well, that's a great theory. But it's wrong—even with one kid, you only get $437 a month. And to live off that, good luck! Even if you're looking for an apartment, that by itself is at least $300 or $400.

"The government says now that they want to solve that problem by having guys report if they get a girl pregnant, if it's their baby. But I say, they can't even get most guys to go in and get a blood test when it's court ordered; how are they going to get a guy to admit he's having sex with someone? I'm lucky we could force David to get a blood test—it came back proving that he's Richard's father. So that will be some assistance from him, I'm hoping.

"I think if you're going to be adult enough to make a baby," she continues confidently, "you should be adult enough either to take care of that baby or to do the right thing, give it up for adoption or whatever. I myself am doing the right thing for my kids. I'm a full-time parent. I've worked outside the home, but it's nothing compared to my job now. I'm up every day at 5:30 in the morning, every day of the year. Whether I get another job to go with that, I got one job all the time, 24-7. So nobody better tell me different.

"Plus, I get tired of how unfair everything is. I mean, David's ex-wife (did I say he'd been married?) had three kids. She hadn't worked in seven years; but the government's never been on her

73

case to get a job. But me? Man, before I got pregnant with Richard, they had me filling out applications left and right!"

"NONE OF THIS IS MY FAULT"

Jamie says she resents being categorized as "just another welfare mom." She says her situation is far different from that of many welfare mothers.

"I told you before, none of this is my fault," she insists. "I know that lots of people think everyone who gets pregnant should have money to send that kid to college, or buy him everything he wants. But some of us can't do that, can't provide those things. There *are* lots of women who have babies for money, to keep getting a bigger welfare check. But that's not me.

"I'm actually proud of myself for being independent. Like when I got pregnant with my oldest, everyone was on my case about not

Jamie takes no responsibility for her current circumstances or her dependence on welfare. "That's the way the system is. . . . It's loaded against us. There's no way out, once you're on welfare."

being able to take care of a baby, that my mom would have to raise him. But you know when the first time my mom ever baby-sat Dean? When I was in labor with Dusty, that's when!

"I *did* consider adoption with Richard," she admits. "But deep down, I knew I couldn't. I'd be avoiding my responsibility. I'm his mother, I'm the one who should be raising him. That's the fact that kept staring me in the face."

Jamie says that ultimately, it is the system's fault that she is on welfare at all.

"I'll tell you why," she says. "Because I'm not well educated. I only went part of the way through ninth grade before I got pregnant with Dean. I only have a fifth-grade reading level, too. But hey, they kept passing me, from sixth grade, to seventh, to eighth and ninth. Now since I quit school, I know ten other people who graduated high school who have lower reading levels than I do!

"They make too much of an issue out of getting jobs. Well, I say, you gotta have jobs that people can do. Well, I've got a fifth-grade reading level. So who's going to hire me? Who? Some factory, I guess, and that's about it. But I'm not going to make much, not even enough to pay for good day care.

"But hey," she says with a bitter laugh. "I guess that's okay. I'll be working, right? And then the people can all say, 'Well, that's one less woman on welfare.' It's stupid. But that's the way the system is. If you take the trouble to look at it, you can see it's loaded against us. There's no way out, once you're on welfare."

"Yeah, I've Had Some Regrets"

As irritated as Jamie gets about the way she thinks she has been treated in the system, she admits that she has wished things had turned out differently.

"I wouldn't change my kids for anything," she says forcefully. "But I will say, yeah, I've had some regrets. I've had moments that I've wished I'd had a little time before they came along. Like when I was pregnant with Richard, I went down to Memphis to see my cousin graduate from high school. While I was there, I helped her get ready for her senior prom. The whole time I'm thinking, 'Yeah, I've got my babies, and I'm glad.' But there was another part of me that was thinking, 'You'll never know what it feels like to go to the prom, either. Is it really what I always wanted—sitting home 24-7 being a mom, or going to the prom?' It made me think.

"And I gotta tell you, it used to get me really resentful when I was pregnant in high school. All my friends would say, 'Oh, we love babies. If you ever need a baby-sitter, let us know.' Right. Which one of you is going to say, 'Oh, I'll cancel my date tonight with John or Joe or whoever, so I can go watch Jamie's baby.'"

Jamie snorts, shaking her head in disgust. "But at the same time, I know I'm pretty darn lucky."

IN THE NEXT FEW YEARS

There is whimpering from the next room, and Jamie tells Dean to go in and get the baby. In a few minutes, he comes back with Richard, red-cheeked and fussy.

"This is my baby," she says, taking the baby. "He's got some health problems, maybe you can tell. His head isn't growing the way it's supposed to. Everything on the inside is getting kind of

"I wouldn't change my kids for anything," Jamie says. "But . . . I've had some regrets," she confides. "I've had moments that I've wished I'd had a little time before they came along."

cone shaped; that's the reason his cheeks are so plump—they're being forced down and out. Everything in his head is growing on the inside, but the outside isn't keeping up. See, feel that," she says, lightly feeling around under the baby's mat of blond hair.

"They're talking about shunting him, kind of a laser thing," she explains. "I'm not really sure what it all means. Medical assistance will help with that, I'm almost positive. We were supposed to go in last Thursday, but the doctor was delivering a baby, so our appointment got changed. But I guess the other option is surgery on his skull, which will leave scars. But they say the scars would get hidden by his hair, eventually. I'm hoping whatever they do, they do it soon. He gets real sore from the pressure of his head—he even gets bruises on his scalp."

Besides the baby's operation, has she set any goals for herself in the next few years? Jamie stares into space a minute, thinking.

"I'd like to get the basement done," she says, smiling. "I want to stay here, stay in this house. I'm getting the house out of the divorce, like I said. And as far as a relationship goes, I don't think I'm looking for one. I guess I don't see a reason to, because I've learned I do better on my own.

"A lot of people think you have to be in a relationship to have kids," she says confidentially. "But believe me, you don't. It's not important for you or the kids. That's the last thing you need. It's the father there, willing to help out occasionally, that's all. I don't need to live with the father, or love him, or anything like that."

"I SEE THEM GOING TO LIVE WITH JERRY"

Jamie says that she can envision her boys wanting to live with Jerry when they get to be twelve or thirteen.

"I see them going to live with Jerry," she says matter-of-factly. "He's got ten acres out where he lives; he's got three-wheelers, a snowmobile, all kinds of fun stuff. They like it there, so maybe I'll let him have the older two when they're older. I haven't decided yet.

"See, I've got to put them first, not myself. This is a little place; even though we're on a lake, we're in the city limits. No three-wheelers allowed around here, stuff like that. I think they'd like being out there with him, living with more space. I can honestly say it would be hard for me, but at least they're only a few miles away, and I could go see them."

Although Jamie buys her clothes at thrift stores and rummage sales to save money, she says she splurges on her sons. "I buy all their clothes new from stores. I won't make them wear other people's old throwaways."

Dean pipes up from the sofa, "Plus the neighbors here are *mean*."

Jamie smiles sadly. "Yeah, the people here have been real jerks to my boys. The neighbor kids call my kids names, look down on them. A lot of it is because we're poor. Like Dusty's friend—Dusty is allowed to play over there, but the kid isn't allowed to come here at all. His parents say there's too many domestic problems here.

"But they can all go to hell, because I'm going to stay here; I'm not leaving. No one's driving us out of here. See, I think a lot of the reason people aren't nice to us is how the house looks. I know it looks real bad, but it honestly doesn't bother me. My priorities are different from other people's.

"See that big house across the street? I know the people who live there, and they scrimped and saved for that big house, to where they don't have any money to do anything else. I don't want to be like that. Already I'm scrimping. I buy all my clothes from the Goodwill or rummage sales. But my boys are different. I buy all their clothes new from stores. I won't make them wear other people's old throwaways. I shop for bargains, but at least they're new."

"WE DON'T USUALLY HAVE TOO MUCH LEFT OVER"

Dean has come over to stand by his mother's chair. He has been listening to the talk of buying clothes.

"Mom, can I get Nikes for back-to-school? Just the $29 ones, please?"

His pleas are drowned out by her quick no's. "Dean, come on, you know we can't get Nikes." She looks at her visitor. "This is when it gets hard, you know? He just wants what the other kids have, that's all. But it's too much for our budget. I expect my kids to understand that, that they can't dress the way everyone else does. But I also understand that they feel bad sometimes. They don't hear too many yes's around here.

"Right now, welfare is keeping us afloat. I get a check every month in the mail for $950. Now, I don't get food stamps any more—the $351 worth of food stamp money is included in that check. The rest of it goes for bills. This month and next month are tight, with school coming up. New shoes, new pants, because they grew out of their jeans over the summer. School supplies, stuff like that. I'm smart about shopping—I get all the stuff when it goes on sale.

"I bought all the new paper, the crayons, the glue—that's all hidden now under Richard's crib. I've had it a few weeks now. I don't want them getting into it before school starts. If I didn't hide it, they'd be playing with it now, especially with the rain and everything."

Jamie admits that the welfare check goes quickly, and rarely is there much left over for splurging.

"Sometimes we have enough left over and we rent a couple movies, order a pizza," she says. "I will do that on a Saturday night sometimes. We have lots of the Disney movies I've bought—I think we've got almost every one," she says, pointing to a crowded shelf next to the television. "But that's it—no vacations, no wild shopping sprees. No designer stuff."

"It's Sometimes Embarrassing"

Does she feel she is treated differently because she is on welfare? Jamie nods emphatically.

"Oh, yeah," she says. "People say to me, 'If you had a better education, if you didn't have so many kids, blah, blah, blah.' I get tired of hearing it. I love being home with my kids. I regret that we need welfare to do it, but hey, that's a fact—deal with it.

"For Jerry, it's real different, because he comes from a pretty rich family. They don't even have a clue about welfare. One time, a long time ago, we were going to barbecue, just have hot dogs and stuff with his family. Well, me and one of his sisters went to the store to get some juice and buns and that, and I went to pay for it, and you should have seen the look! That's back when we used actual food stamps, you know? And his sister says, real snotty like, 'Oh, we didn't know you guys got assistance.' I thought, 'You b——!'

"But on the other hand, I can understand a lot of the questions people have. I have some of my own, because there's a lot of no-good welfare women out there. I had a friend who was pregnant with her fifth or sixth girl, I can't remember. And she's had a bunch more kids since then. Well, the kids got on a Christmas wish list, you know, for kids to donate things that poor families need?

"Well, all her kids got nice jackets and you know what this woman did? She took the jackets into the store and got the money! I thought that was horrible. How can you get pregnant, carry a baby for nine months, and take his coat in because you need the money more? No, you don't. A baby needs his coat."

She says that her kids, too, have been on Christmas wish lists, which has really been helpful. She tells Dean to go into the closet and get his good coat. He scampers off, happy to be part of the discussion.

"There was a wish list last Christmas at his school," she says, taking the thick jade-colored Columbia jacket from his hands. "Look at this—it's beautiful! I mean, Dean had a coat, but it was real shabby. I was so surprised that someone would spend this kind of money on a wish list kid. And he got a hat, too, a real pretty green one to match the coat.

"Sure, he felt a little funny about it. I mean, that's human nature. Nobody wants to admit that they're poor. But Dean is so proud of his coat, and he takes real good care of it. Look at this, a lifetime warranty!"

"I GOT MORE GOALS, TOO"

Jamie walks to the counter for a cookie for Richard, who has resumed his fussing.

"I was thinking about what you were saying before, about goals. Well, I was thinking that I got more goals, too. I think I interrupted myself before about the people in the fancy house across the street. But I want my boys to always be warm in the winter—good coats and hats. I don't want to be eating cereal for dinner just to have a pretty house.

"I admit, when I was a little girl, I didn't think I'd grow up and live in a dump like this. I guess I wanted a pretty house, with fresh

Despite Jamie's uncertain future, she is hopeful that her children will do well in school so that they can obtain well-paying jobs and break the welfare cycle.

paint, lots of windows. But this is life. I don't have a house like that. I probably never will, and I got to accept that. It isn't important to me anymore. The biggest thing for me now is that nice feeling in the morning, just before I get out of bed. Knowing I'll be here with them, raising them. Hoping they do good in school.

"And that's another goal, hoping they do better than me. I want them to learn to read and enjoy it. Dusty's getting help at summer school for his reading. Dean's pretty good; he just needs to learn to concentrate on getting his work done. But they're both smart. I'm hoping that they grow up and can get good jobs. They don't need to be getting welfare like me."

Kathy

"I HAVE A GOAL FOR THIS FALL—I
WANT TO GET ANOTHER JOB, SO
I CAN GET BACK THAT FEELING I
HAD WHEN I WAS WORKING."

Author's Note: Kathy applied for welfare when she became pregnant in her junior year of high school. Now divorced with four children, she has collected assistance for medical bills, food, rent, and other expenses. For one period of time—the happiest in her life, she says—she was working full-time and was off welfare. Now, at thirty-four, she finds herself receiving another kind of assistance—a Social Security check for her vision impairment.

"God, what a mess!" comes a voice from just inside the back door. "I'm sorry—come around to the front, will you? The toilet just overflowed or something upstairs, and water's pouring down everywhere!"

At the front door there is a hurried clicking of locks and the door is opened by a stoic-faced little boy of about nine. His mom, he says softly, is washing her hands and will be right in. In a few moments, a slight, pretty young woman in a robin's egg blue warmup suit walks into the room. She is followed closely by a golden Lab of indeterminate age. Tripping on the leg of the coffee table, she lurches forward onto the sofa and sits down.

"I'm Kathy," she says, flashing a quick smile. "And I'm really sorry I'm so late. It's my thirty-fourth birthday today and my toilet upstairs decided to explode. Great birthday, huh?"

She leans over and pats the dog. "This is Porsche; she's my second set of eyes. I'm vision-impaired, you know. She's my boyfriend's

83

dog, really, not trained as a Seeing Eye dog or anything, but she's amazing! She's taken me on as her personal project, I think."

A CITY GIRL

Kathy is on welfare—has been, she says, most of the time since 1981, when her oldest son, Tony, was born.

"I was not raised on welfare, no," she says. "When I registered back then for medical assistance, that was my introduction to welfare. My family wasn't rich or well-off or anything, but I never felt deprived of anything, you know? When you're a kid, you just figure your parents are taking care of you, and mine did. I was happy, and I never thought about how much money we had or didn't

Kathy holds a small tape recorder during her interview. Although she was not raised on welfare, Kathy has been accepting aid periodically since 1981, when her oldest child was born.

have. There were seven girls in our family and one boy—a blended family, since each of my parents had been married before. Plus, they had three of their own. My dad was a bus driver, and we lived in the city.

"Like lots and lots of women on welfare, I started in the system as a pregnant teenager. I was seventeen, a junior in high school. We had moved from the city to a big suburb. I absolutely hated it. I was a city girl, pure and simple. I had always lived in a racially mixed neighborhood. I'm biracial—you maybe didn't know that, because I'm real fair, but my dad is French Canadian and black, and my mom is white.

"So I was really comfortable in the neighborhood we had in the city. I think we moved because my dad wanted to give my mom a nice house in the suburbs. He wanted to get us out of the city; I'm not sure of the reasons. I know my mom always wanted a new home, and that's what she got when we moved."

"I WAS MISS POPULAR WHERE I WAS"

Kathy says that the move was traumatic for her.

"I was Miss Popular where I was, coming from a small Catholic grade school. Everybody knew everybody, and friends were everywhere. I went from first grade to eighth grade there, so it was a comfort zone for me. So when we moved, it was hard.

"I was scared, insecure, and very withdrawn. I didn't know how to make friends very well. A lot of it was the fact that it was so *white*. I think it was weird for my dad, too. I mean, when the realtors dealt with him on the phone—because his voice doesn't have what people think of as a 'black' sound—they were very enthusiastic. But when we showed up, and they saw he was black, they told him the land was sold. It was really shameful, I thought. Eventually, though, he got the land he wanted, and we moved in.

"The pregnancy came about really because of the move. I really missed the city, and my mom would drive me back there every weekend to stay with my old friends. My mom was really nice about that. My older sister had a boyfriend back in the city, and she fixed me up with her boyfriend's little brother. His name was Joe, and I really fell in love with him.

"I look back on it now, and I see that I really clung to him," she says. "It was teenage love. I'd go from my Monday through Friday home to the city on weekends, and my happiness was there, with him. I hadn't been sexually active at all until him, and I ended up pregnant."

PREGNANT AND ALONE

Although she says her parents were disappointed and hurt at first, they rallied to support her.

"My mom and I had always been real close, and I knew she'd come around," says Kathy. "She had been pregnant herself at seventeen, but married—that was a whole different thing.

"But Joe was a different story. His family was adamant that I terminate the pregnancy. That made me really angry. I was seventeen and they were taking charge of my life, and I was resentful. But they didn't give in; they moved him out of state—they all went. I didn't see him my whole pregnancy. Joe tried a little to keep in touch, but we really didn't connect at all.

Because of her declining eyesight, Kathy now depends on Porsche, her boyfriend's dog, to help her get around.

"The fact is, by the time he contacted me, my mom was really supportive. I was enrolled in a teenage parent program at my school; I was attending classes. Really, I didn't need him anymore. By the time my due date came, Joe had come back, and I didn't even want to see him. It's strange; we'd gone from love, to pregnancy, to nothing. I guess he chose a critical time to leave—his actions really spoke louder than any words could."

"She Wanted to Teach Me a Lesson"

During her pregnancy, Kathy's mother had been a real source of strength for her, she says.

"She threw me a baby shower and everything," laughs Kathy. "By the time Tony was born, I had everything any baby could possibly want. She also urged me to follow through on the welfare I'd been told about in my parenting classes.

"I hadn't really taken it seriously. Back then you could apply two months before the baby came, to get your crib, your supplies, and everything together. I don't think they pay out nowadays before the baby is born, but back then they did. But like I said, my mom had given me that baby shower, so I thought, 'What do I need welfare for?'

"Well, my mom told me that even if I didn't need it, I should sign up anyway. I remember thinking, 'Wow, free money!' I never really thought about it, but it was nice having it around. I bought him some little outfits, just things I wanted. I also remember thinking, 'This isn't going to be so hard at all.' Boy, what a shock I was in for.

"As soon as Tony was born, my mom started charging me rent. I couldn't believe it—my own mother. And another thing is that she wouldn't baby-sit him. She loved him—he was the apple of her eye—but she wouldn't watch him. Now, I see what she was doing, that she was doing it for a reason. She wanted to teach me a lesson. This wasn't a game; I wasn't playing dolls. Now I think it was smart, her charging me $200. That was most of my welfare check. In her mind, I was eating there, doing laundry. But then, I was really mad, and I got a real attitude with her."

A Difficult Transition

Kathy's irritation with her mother was compounded by her own feelings of being too young to be a mother. In the first months of Tony's life, she felt strange in that role.

"I'd gone too fast from childhood to womanhood," she says flatly. "I know that. I wasn't ready at all to be a mother; I was still kind of a baby. Kind of? I guess my younger sister and I *were* babies—we were so coddled and protected. I loved Tony, and I wouldn't let him out of my sight. But I didn't think of myself as a mom. In fact, the first time he called me 'mama' I thought I would die. I thought, 'I'm not a mama!'

"I stayed at home, though, paying my rent, going to school. School was one thing I really wanted to complete. I didn't want a GED [general equivalency diploma], I wanted the diploma, the real thing. It was hard, though. I felt so different from the others. I wasn't doing the parties, the dances. But I hung in there—even got on the B honor roll—and got the diploma.

"But when I was eighteen I moved in with my brother. He had a little apartment in the city, and he was more than happy to have me and Tony there, too. I had food stamps, my little check for bills, I was covered. We split the rent, and we had fun for a couple of years.

LIVING ON WELFARE

In those days, Kathy says, she got a check for bills and a separate pack of food stamps that she could use in grocery stores. Today, however, she receives neither—she now has what looks like a plastic credit card.

"It's like a Visa or whatever," she says, fishing it out of her wallet. "It's great—I love it. It's a much better system. See, it has a little magnetic strip on the back, just like a credit card. You just go to the store and slide it through the machine, and push your code. And then you push the button for either food stamps or cash. It reads out your balance.

"Like, if I was going to use it now, it would tell me that I have about $25 left in my food stamp account. And if my bill came to $10, then it would print out the new balance of $15. You always know how much you have, and you can't go over. The other thing is that it's safe—you can't get robbed, because the only way it works is if the person knows your secret code, and you don't go giving that out. If you lose the card, or it gets stolen, they'll replace it right away.

"I can use it at a regular cash machine, too. Like if I want to pay for my kids' shoes in cash, I can get the amount out of there, provided that I have enough in the account."

At the grocery store, Kathy uses a sort of credit card to check the balance of her welfare account.

But how does the system make sure that people don't abuse the card—use cash meant for bills or rent to purchase drugs or lottery tickets, for instance? Kathy shakes her head.

"I don't think you can safeguard against that, not really," she says. "I don't really think that too many people are going to be taking food out of their kids' mouths doing that. I'm sure that there's a handful, because we know there are real crazy people in this world, but not many. But the advantages of this system work way better than the old way of food stamps, believe me."

"ONCE YOU'VE GOT THEM IN YOUR POCKET, WATCH OUT"

Kathy says the old method of payment with food stamps was tremendously risky, and was the source of a lot of problems for welfare recipients.

"There was nothing personal about them, like with the cash card," she explains. "No account number or anything. I think maybe there was some code, but it would have been almost impossible for anyone to trace them if they were stolen. And they were *always* getting stolen. Not just from me, from lots of people. Once you've got them in your pocket, watch out. I've gotten them ripped off many times.

"People knew when the checks and food stamps arrived in the mail, see," she says. "They'd steal them right out of mailboxes. And I've had them taken out of my purse at home by baby-sitters. Lots of times it was people in the neighborhood, people who knew you. It was creepy, really an odd feeling. Really, it was a bad system.

"Plus, I'll tell you another reason they were bad. The welfare recipients themselves sometimes committed fraud. I never did this, but I knew it was done. See, if your check or your food stamps were stolen, the government would replace them. So people were reporting them stolen when they weren't, so they'd get double the money."

BUYING EXTRAS

Food stamp thieves didn't necessarily want the stamps to purchase food, either. Much of the time, they were sold on the black market for cash to buy drugs or liquor.

"The value on the street is half of what they're worth," she says. "Like, if you give someone $200 worth of food stamps, it's like $100 in cash. I don't know why that is, but it is. Truthfully, I've purchased food stamps like that. Give someone $50 and get $100 worth of groceries—it was a survival thing, a good deal. I didn't think about it being illegal back then. I figured if someone was selling them, they just didn't need them. Now, of course, you know that people were using the money to party, especially with crack. You could buy lots of crack with $50. But then it was very, very common, and people were doing it like crazy."

Nowadays, says Kathy, the welfare system has gotten far more sophisticated; more often suspicion of fraud triggers investigations. But she explains that she likes the new system for another reason besides its safety.

"It was embarrassing," she says simply. "You felt like you had this big sign on your back or something when you used food

Kathy and her son shop for groceries. Kathy says that changes to the welfare system have helped safeguard against the food stamp fraud and theft that used to plague the system.

stamps—WELFARE MOM. At first, I didn't get it—I was too young and stupid. Like I said, I thought the idea of free money was really cool at first. Of course, in the suburbs where we lived, I learned real fast how people treated you. They'd give you the look, you know, the haughty stare. Or they acted disgusted. I'm talking about the clerks in the stores. They'd look down their noses, and they'd say, 'Food stamps? Well, *you'll* have to rip them out of the book.'"

She didn't get that reaction in the city, she says, but in the suburb where her parents lived, it was intolerable.

"Even my dad and mom were embarrassed using them," she remembers. "Like if they were going to the store, and I asked them to get some baby food or whatever. I'd give them food stamps to cover it, and they'd say no. And girlfriends would offer to get me things, and I'd offer my stamps. 'No,' they'd say. 'Nothing personal, but that's too embarrassing.' I figured it out, too.

"When I moved to the city to live at my brother's, it was no big deal, especially in the inner city. I'd just ask, 'Do you take food stamps?' and they'd say yes or no. Lots and lots of people were in the same boat as me, so I felt fine about it there."

LIFE WITH RHONDA

After living with her brother for almost two years, Kathy and Tony moved in with a friend named Rhonda.

"She was a great friend," smiles Kathy. "We actually met because we were both in love with the same guy—he was two-timing both of us against each other! But our friendship outlasted him, luckily. We got along great and thought of ourselves as sisters, basically. Anyway, we found a little one-bedroom efficiency, a little rattrap. Yikes, I think of that place now, with the bugs and roaches, and I'm amazed we did it. I'd never lived with bugs before. I guess we were so excited to be on our own, no family living with us, that we treated the whole thing as an adventure. We were young, and that helps a lot.

"We were caretakers in our apartment building, so that knocked $100 off our rent. Rhonda had a job, I was getting my check and my food stamps, and we were scraping by. Plus, that's the time in my life when I discovered food shelves. Boy, that helped us a lot! We cut corners any way we could, even washing our clothes in the tub. Again, it was like camping or something, so I loved it. And when we were really broke, my mom and dad and her mom, they'd help out with groceries once in a while. We had a safety net, so that was cool."

During that time Kathy's application for public housing came through, and she got her first house.

"It was great," she says. "I had applied back when Tony was a newborn for subsidized public housing. But you know, those lists are really long. So we moved to this great duplex in the south of the city. It was actually really close to the Catholic school that I'd gone to when I was a little girl, so I was excited.

"And the house! It was great—clean, no bugs, nothing. The rent worked on a sliding scale. You paid 30 percent of whatever your income was. Rhonda moved with me and Tony; she wasn't really supposed to, but we did it anyway. We were buddies."

RHONDA MOVES OUT

Rhonda had a job as a nurse at a nearby nursing home and was busy all the time. Kathy, however, found that her life was becoming boring.

"I wanted to work, to do something," she says. "I had Tony, but I missed the way things were before with me and Rhonda, going out, doing things. But she was busier with her new job. I was lonely.

"Money wasn't stretching like it was before, either. Prices were going up, and Tony was growing and needed new clothes. And being bored, I was yearning for more things. I wanted to shop just

Kathy and her son carry bags of groceries home from the supermarket. Because Kathy is supported by welfare, she and her family are eligible for subsidized public housing.

to do something, but that was out of the question for me. I just didn't have the money. More and more, I remember Rhonda was carrying me, especially by the end of the month. She never said anything; she was glad to do it. I didn't want to sponge off her, but what could I do?

"After a while, she started dating a guy, and she ended up moving out. That was hard for me. I was resentful of the guy, because I missed her. I remember one time she came back to see me, and I was telling her how broke and lonesome I was. Well, at that time she had a nursing job and she had gotten into stripping at a place downtown. I was just appalled; I couldn't believe it.

"But she kept saying, 'Kathy—you should do it. I'm making so much money, and you could, too.' But I was shocked. I loved her like a sister, but I really disapproved. And I thought I could never do anything like that! But there she was, pushing me, pushing me. And she showed me the roll of bills she had, and I got to admit, I was impressed."

"I Had to Think of It as an Art"

Kathy finally agreed to go with Rhonda to the bar downtown, just to see for herself what it was like.

"I saw that it was all behind glass," she says. "Just a peep show. And I loved to dance. When I was little, that's what I was going to do when I grew up. But I was so modest. I saw Rhonda go into this little glass room and start dancing, and I couldn't believe it.

"The manager was there, and he said, 'You want to jump in and try? I said no. But Rhonda just kept talking to me, telling me to try it one time, and I finally did. It was two-way mirrors—I forgot to say that. That made it easier. I don't think I could have stood seeing the men on the other side. So I walked through the curtain and started dancing.

"And all of a sudden, this money came through these slots in the wall, into the little room where we were. And Rhonda says, 'That's for you.' I went, 'No way!' But she said, 'Hey, you've already done it—now there's nothing to it. What have you got to lose?' And I guess she was right.

"Well, I really changed my mind. I met the girls, met everybody. I had thought they'd all be whores or something, but they weren't. They were students, mothers, nurses, people just like me. So I kept doing it, but I had to think of it as an art, not stripping. That would have been too weird. I told myself I was safe, because no one I knew would go to a place like that, so I'd never be recognized. My father, my brothers—never!

"So I kept it up. It was cash only, so I didn't report it to the welfare office. I know I should have, but the money was great, and I didn't want to give it up. I paid for my own day care—one of the other girls at the club worked a different shift, so she watched Tony until I came home, and then she went to work."

RUSHING INTO MARRIAGE

Her stripping career did not last, however. The friend who had been watching Tony thought she was going to be late for her shift, and brought Tony with her to work.

"I've never been so angry," Kathy says. "I was so mad. She was so worried about missing a little money that she brought him, even though I'd told her I never *never* wanted Tony near that place. My

Kathy worked as a stripper for a short time to supplement her welfare payments. Although she liked the profits from stripping, Kathy says shame got the best of her.

reality just snapped. Everybody was in the dressing room, and I'm hearing Tony's voice saying, 'Mom, Mom.' Oh, man—I'd had my two worlds so separated, but at the moment they just collided. I'd been trying to protect him, but I couldn't. I was so ashamed.

"I had reservations about the job after that. I wasn't as excited about it; I was working fewer shifts. And what happened was, I met a guy, a friend of a friend. His name was Andre, and he was really great. He had a daughter by another relationship, and he was such a good father to her. I thought I'd really like to be with someone like him. I was young and dumb," she says, shaking her head.

Kathy got pregnant, and soon quit her job at the club. When she told her parents she was expecting another baby, they were devastated.

"My mom was so mad at me at first, she wouldn't speak to me," says Kathy. "The first pregnancy she chalked up to me being young, just a mistake. But this was too much. And my dad was really sad, too. I think they both thought of my pregnancy as an indication that I hadn't gotten any more sense than I'd had at seventeen. And I felt really bad, terribly bad.

"Danielle was my baby girl; she was born in January. Feeling so guilty about my parents, I pushed for Andre and I to get married soon afterwards. We did, too, that June. It was a big mistake. I was legally with him until just a month ago, and that all wasn't peaches and cream, let me tell you. But three lovely children came out of that marriage—and that was the only good."

"It Started Like a Pinkeye Infection"

Early in her marriage to Andre, Kathy woke up one morning with what seemed like an eye infection.

"It was hard to open my lids, you know—it started like a pinkeye infection," she says. "Both eyes burned and felt real uncomfortable. I went to my clinic, my regular doctor. He gave me some eyedrops, but they didn't work. And the doctor didn't seem to know what else to do—he was baffled. I was panicking, because although the burning and the matting was going away, my vision was blurry.

"I went to the University Hospital, to specialists there. I had about a year's worth of tests, too—dye shot into my eyes, you name it. Whatever it was took vision with it, and that was scary.

The doctors knew that the swelling of my eye was cutting off the optic nerve. I could still read, could still drive.

"I didn't want to hear that the doctors believed it would get progressively worse. They weren't even sure about that, and they admitted it. But even if they had been sure, I wouldn't have accepted it. I went in every two or three weeks for evaluations, and they put me on a drug called prednisone. My medical assistance paid for it, for all the tests and everything.

"It wasn't a problem all the time. It would flare up sometimes—I think stress made it worse—and I'd get injections in my eyes. I dealt with it, I guess. Each time, though, the doctors would tell me that according to their tests I was losing a little more vision. I could

Kathy holds her walking cane while she waits at the bus stop near her home. Her vision became impaired shortly after the birth of her second child.

still drive, but it was harder. I found myself printing and writing a little larger, too. I couldn't always recognize people I met on the street, and that was frustrating."

THE CAUSE OF THE STRESS

Kathy says that she was told by her doctors that stress would not only make her medical problem worse but also impede the drug's effectiveness. She knew she had a great deal of stress in her life, and the cause was very clear to her.

"My marriage was very stressful," she says. "I'd had another baby with him, named Andre Jr. I had three—Tony, Danielle, and little Andre—and I loved my kids. But Andre was becoming abusive, not the man I thought I married. He was drinking a lot, using drugs a lot. Before, he'd drunk a little beer, smoked a little pot (though never around me, because I didn't like it). But now it was more and more, and he was rough with me. I covered it up with my parents, because I didn't want them to think I'd screwed up again.

"He wasn't working full-time at anything. He drove an ice cream truck for a little while, and there was the occasional janitorial job. But mostly we lived off my welfare check. I had medical assistance, and we got more money for each kid. We had public housing, so we were getting by."

Kathy says that although she was supposed to report that she was married, she never did.

"I must have been having premonitions or something," she says with a smile. "I mean, maybe I always knew we wouldn't stay together, I don't know. He never had a job—and when he did a little part-time thing, we never saw any of the money. He'd go out drinking and just blow it, you know? And if I lost the welfare, the kids and I would be in a terrible fix. So I guess it was fraud, but in another way, I was being very honest about what we needed."

THE MOST WONDERFUL TIME

There was one point during the worst of her marriage, Kathy says, when she was probably the happiest she'd ever been in her life.

"I was able to get off welfare," she beams. "It felt so good, you can't even imagine. I wanted to work, I wanted to get active. Just being home with the kids, being around Andre and his abuse, it was awful. I felt like I was just waiting around to go blind. I was twenty-three, and Andre was my baby. I needed to get us all out of the house, away from Andre. I figured it was time to get more in my life, to look for a job.

"A girlfriend of mine had found a job in the paper, a janitorial job at Courage Center, a spot for handicapped people. Everyone there was like me, had some sort of disability. Some were in wheelchairs, some using canes, whatever. It was the best thing in the world for me, just the best!

"It was a real confidence builder for me, let me tell you. I was making good money. I called the welfare office right away and said, 'I'm history, take me off right now.' Man, what a feeling," she laughs. "I still got some food stamps, and day care, though—they told me I was still eligible for those. I took my kids to a day care in a church right near the house, and they loved it. Lots of toys, lots of kids to play with.

"I worked forty hours a week, cleaning. I started out at $5.50 an hour, and gradually worked myself up to $8.50. The people there knew about my vision—I'd been real up front about that. They even helped me out, covered for me with the various chemicals for cleaning there, so I knew what I was using all the time. I had paid vacations, and even my own insurance, for the first time in my life. I was so proud of myself."

"IT WAS A KILLER, THOUGH"

As good as it felt to be almost completely self-supporting, Kathy remembers that the days were long.

"I loved it, but it was a killer, though," she says. "I was up at 5 in the morning to get the kids dressed and out the door so we could be at day care by 6. I took a bus to work, got there by 7. I worked until 3:30, and took a bus home to get the kids and get home. The minute I was home, it was cook dinner, read to them, do laundry, clean, whatever. I was fried. And this husband of mine was worthless—no help there. I was so worn out some days that I'd fall asleep on the couch in my clothes.

"It was so good for me, though. I love to talk to people, and there were so many interesting people there at the center. All day long, meeting people who had lives that were far harder than mine; it put things into perspective for me. I was a good worker, and the staff recognized it. I even had some of the bigwigs there on the board of directors approach me about cleaning their houses for some extra money."

Now divorced from her violent husband, Kathy says that she and her four children are eager for a fresh start. "We're still on welfare," she says, "but there are some changes coming."

The bubble burst, however, when Kathy discovered she was pregnant again.

"It was so strange," she says with embarrassment. "Andre and I hadn't been speaking most of the time. The one time we were intimate, I guess that was all it took. I started going into premature labor, and that was the end of work for me. The doctor wanted me to slow way down. Not that staying at home with kids eight, four, and two would be slowing down, but I guess it was not as much physical labor as working at the center. I love Nicholas dearly, but I call him my miracle baby—I don't know how he survived all those premature labors that I had. I guess he just hung in there, huh?"

THE END OF THE LINE

Home all day again, Kathy knew her life with Andre had to end soon.

"I had four kids, a no-good husband, and awful vision," she says. "I got the kids active in as much stuff at the park as I could. We did Cub Scouts, Brownies, hockey, you name it. Anything to get them away from the monster. And believe me, he had really turned into one.

"The kids weren't physically abused. But verbally and emotionally, yes. Being away from it, I can look back and say they were damaged, probably more from just hearing him abuse me. He was cheating on me with my baby-sitter—I found *that* out from the neighborhood kids. He'd drink or do crack, and then he'd get psychotic, break up everything in the house.

"He'd just snap, I don't know. He'd bust up tables, chairs, furniture, anything. He'd shake me around like a rag doll. I had bruises all over me, all of the time. My vision took another dive, no big surprise, I guess because of all the stress. I don't honestly think he even knew what he was doing. He'd sometimes wake up the next morning, and he'd say, 'Hi, honey,' like he didn't have a clue why I was upset.

"I'd stay up all night after one of his explosions, trying to put things back together so the kids weren't scared when they saw the mess. But I was stupid, because even if they didn't see it, they heard the noise. The damage was done. I couldn't protect them by covering it up. I knew we had to get rid of him; he was destroying me and the kids, too. We got divorced. In fact, it just became all legal and done about five weeks ago."

"I DON'T WANT TO BE IN THE DARK BEFORE MY TIME"

Kathy feels very positive about her life now. She and her children have moved just a few blocks from where they lived with Andre.

"It feels good to start fresh, to have a new start," she says. "This house is great, and we're in basically the same neighborhood as we were before. I was able to get the house on my Section 8, my public housing assistance. We're still on welfare, but there are some changes coming, I think.

Kathy now receives disability payments because of her vision impairment. Every month she receives a disability check for five hundred dollars, and the government pays for all of her vision-related expenses.

"First of all, my vision deteriorated to the point where I became eligible for some disability. It's I think 20/200 in one eye and 20/100 in the other; 20/20 is normal, of course. I'm light sensitive; sometimes I can see things, sometimes I can't. I usually go by sound, to tell you the truth. And I kind of slide along when I'm in the house, just so I don't trip on a shoe or a rug or even a toy that one of the kids left out.

"But the government gives me a good deal with that disability check. In addition to paying me $500 a month, they'll pick up the cost of vision aids like binoculars, magnifiers, even computer hookups. I don't know how bad my vision will get; the doctors aren't sure themselves. I know that all my life I'll be on that medication to keep the swelling down. I'm hoping it will stay where it is, and not get worse, but we'll see.

"A couple of years ago I went to the School for the Blind, to learn to use the cane, learn Braille, the whole thing, just in case, you know. It's funny, because in a way all that blind training made me feel more handicapped. I became more of what I didn't want to be, and I don't want to be in the dark before my time. I got hooked on the cane, and I started accepting my limitations, and I don't think that was right.

"I don't want to put it down, because I think if I'd been totally blind, it would have been great. But I didn't want to use my cane all the time, because in reality I don't have to—yet. Braille was fun, though—like learning Spanish or something. But once I was done with that School for the Blind, I put the cane away. With Porsche here, maybe I'll have a Seeing Eye dog, who knows?

"THE KIDS LOVE HIM"

Kathy is also optimistic about her future with her boyfriend, Marcus.

"He's great," she says happily. "He looks like a bodybuilder, real strong, but he's a teddy bear, and the kids love him. He's very work oriented, but right now *he's* on disability, too—talk about coincidence! He's always worked in construction, things like that. He got hurt on the job not long ago, hurt his shoulder. He's had surgery, and he's hoping that it will heal fast so he can get back to work.

"We're talking about getting married, and that would be great. With my disability, and his income from his construction job, we'd be off welfare, and that would be wonderful!"

Kathy takes a deep breath and looks as though she is fighting tears.

"The biggest issue in my life right now is that my mom was recently diagnosed with lung cancer. I don't know how it will turn out for her, but it's really upsetting to me. She's been so good to me all these years, and so forgiving, even when I made her mad.

Marcus has been really supportive, because he knows I'm feeling bad right now.

"And I guess the last thing is that I have a goal for this fall—I want to get another job, so I can get back that feeling I had when I was working at the Courage Center. I'd like to get some training as a court reporter or stenographer. I'm not sure if I could do those things if and when I go completely blind. But I could now. And I want to do as much as I can now. So if I go to school and learn how to do it, then get a job, I'll feel like I've really accomplished what I set out to do. I'll be proud of myself."

Epilogue

In the months since these four women were interviewed for this book, there have been some changes in their lives. Twyla is no longer at the shelter; although confidentiality laws prohibit workers there from giving out personal information, an acquaintance says that Twyla and Eddie may be moving up north to be with the rest of their family.

Erin is working hard at school, and she continues to work at the gas station. In addition, Erin has gotten a part-time job working as a security officer, and she volunteers one day a week at a battered women's shelter.

Jamie's news is far less positive. During the birthday party for her son Dusty, her former husband, Jerry, attacked her. In a statement given to the police, Dusty explained that even though Jerry had hit his mother before, this was the first time that she could not stay on her feet. Jamie now has a restraining order against Jerry.

Kathy and her boyfriend, Marcus, are soon to be married, and Kathy says her whole family (including her children) is delighted. She is also scheduled for eye surgery; doctors are hopeful that the surgery will stop the degeneration that has taken place.

Organizations to Contact

American Public Welfare Association
810 First St. NE, Suite 500
Washington, DC 20002

This agency monitors federal and state legislation and regulations and disseminates information to its membership of social welfare administrators and professionals.

Center for Law and Social Policy
1616 P St. NW, Suite 150
Washington, DC 20036

A public interest law firm that engages in policy research and advocacy on behalf of low-income families.

Institute for Research on Poverty
1180 Observatory Dr., 3412 Social Science Building
University of Wisconsin–Madison
Madison, WI 53706

A national center researching the causes and consequences of poverty and social inequality.

National Coalition for the Homeless
1439 Rhode Island Ave. NW
Washington, DC 20005

Offers information on legal support for women and children who are homeless.

For Further Reading

Jill Duerr Berrick, *Faces of Poverty: Portraits of Women and Children on Welfare*. New York: Oxford University Press, 1995. Good information on the history of welfare in the United States.

Joan J. Johnson, *Kids Without Homes*. New York: Franklin Watts, 1991. Helpful information on the hardships of living in subsidized housing.

Robert Lavelle, ed., *America's New War on Poverty*. San Francisco: KQED Books, 1995. Excellent source, with illustrations, graphs, and firsthand accounts of welfare recipients.

Milton Meltzer, *Poverty in America*. New York: William Morrow, 1986. Good section on what can be done to fight poverty in the United States.

Ralph da Costa Nuñez, *The New Poverty: Homeless Families in America*. New York: Plenum Press, 1996. Valuable information on the role of education in combating poverty.

Valerie Polakow, *Lives on the Edge: Single Mothers and Their Children in the Other America*. Chicago: University of Chicago Press, 1993. Highly readable accounts of welfare mothers; excellent index.

Ruth Sidel, *Keeping Women and Children Last: America's War on the Poor*. New York: Penguin Books, 1996. Excellent chapter on children who receive welfare and its effect on them.

Index

earnings affect amount
received, 41–42
is difficult to receive, 92
procedures for receiving,
51–53

teenagers
as mothers, 12–13
therapy, 24–25
Twyla (welfare mother), 14
attitude toward welfare,
30–32, 38
average day of, 33–36
children of, 17, 25, 28–29
plan to live with older
sister, 27, 29–30
relationship with father, 25
employment of, 10, 21–22,
23–24
housing of, 17–19, 26–27, 33
Native American heritage of,
17–21

pregnancies of, 21
relationship with Edward,
22–25
shopping habits of, 36–37

unemployment, 10, 12

welfare
abuse of, 31–32, 46, 73–74
history of, 10–11
laws, 13, 32–33, 51
opposition to, 12
by welfare mothers, 13–14
reform, 12, 13, 32
welfare mothers, 11
attitudes toward, 9–10, 12–14
stereotypes of, 55
women, role of, 10
Women with Infant Children
(WIC), 46

ABOUT THE AUTHOR

Gail B. Stewart is the author of more than eighty books for children and young adults. She lives in Minneapolis, Minnesota, with her husband Carl and their sons Ted, Elliot, and Flynn. When she is not writing, she spends her time reading, walking, and watching her sons play soccer.

Although she has enjoyed working on each of her books, she says that *The Other America* series has been especially gratifying. "So many of my past books have involved extensive research," she says, "but most of it has been library work—journals, magazines, books. But for these books, the main research has been very human. Spending the day with a little girl who has AIDS, or having lunch in a soup kitchen with a homeless man—these kinds of things give you insight that a library alone just can't match."

Stewart hopes that readers of this series will experience some of the same insights—perhaps even being motivated to use some of the suggestions at the end of each book to become involved with someone of the Other America.

About the Photographer

Twenty-two-year-old Theodore E. Roseen currently attends Hamline University in St. Paul, Minnesota, and is studying secondary education in social studies. He has been a photographer for the university's student newspaper, *The Oracle*, for more than three years.